The Open University

CW01621677

Christianity

Units 3–4

Prepared for the course team by

Terry Thomas and J.F. Coakley

A213 World Religions **Arts: a second-level course**

The Open University
Walton Hall, Milton Keynes, MK7 6AA

First published 1987. Reprinted 1990. Second edition 1997. Reprinted 1999.

Edited, designed and typeset by The Open University

Printed in the United Kingdom by Bell and Bain, Glasgow

ISBN 07492 87233

This text is a component of the Open University course A213 *World Religions*. Details of this and other Open University courses are available from Course Enquiries Data Service, PO Box 625, Dane Road, Milton Keynes MK1 1TY, telephone 01908 858585.

16134B/a213u3-4i2.2

Contents

Introductory notes **5**

PART ONE: THE ORIGINS AND HISTORY OF THE CHRISTIAN RELIGION **6**

1 A global perspective **6**

1.1 The Christian religion in today's world 6

1.2 The Christian religion: uniformity or plurality? 7

2 Jesus **9**

2.1 Jesus and Christianity 9

2.2 The gospels 9

2.3 What did Jesus preach? 11

2.4 Jesus Christ, Son of God 13

2.5 The death of Jesus 14

2.6 The Resurrection 16

3 Orthodoxy and heresy **18**

3.1 Heresy 18

3.2 The Trinity 19

3.3 Christology and incarnation 20

3.4 The East–West schism 22

4 Religious life: the outlines **23**

4.1 Baptism 23

4.2 The eucharist 24

4.3 Church order and ministry 26

4.4 Ascetics and monks 27

5 The Christian religion in the modern world **29**

5.1 The Protestant Reformations 31

5.1.1 The German Reformation 31

5.1.2 The Swiss Reformations 32

5.1.3 The radical reformers 34

5.1.4 The English Reformation 34

5.1.5 The Encyclopedia articles 35

5.2 The Christian religion after the Reformation 38

PART TWO: CHRISTIANITY AS A WORLD RELIGION **41**

6 General considerations **41**

6.1 Institutions and organizations 41

6.2 Message, messenger and medium 42

6.3 Sacred writings 43

6.4 The unity of the church 44
6.5 The church: the One Body 45
6.6 The 'Church' and the churches 46
6.7 Church order 47

7 Religious leadership **50**
7.1 Sacred persons 50
7.2 The priesthood 50
7.3 Post-Reformation ministries 53
7.4 Women in the priesthood 57
7.5 Clerics and the laity 57

8 Worship and ritual **59**
8.1 Sacred space 60
8.2 Sacred action and sacred time 60
8.3 Life-cycle rites 65

9 Moral theology and Christian ethics **67**
9.1 The sources of moral/ethical judgement 68
9.2 The ethics of Paul 69
9.3 Law and grace 70
9.4 Moral issues: selected examples 71
9.4.1 The Christian and war 71
9.4.2 Marriage and divorce 72
9.4.3 Contraception 74
9.4.4 Medical termination of pregnancy 75
9.4.5 Homosexuality 76

10 Conclusion **78**

11 Key issues **80**

References **81**

Introductory notes

In conjunction with these units, you should read the articles on Christianity in Zaehner's *Encyclopedia*,[1] in which you will find extensive coverage of the main Christian traditions. In addition to following up references to the *Encyclopedia* in these units, you may also find it helpful to use these articles for background historical information relating to periods in the development of the broader Christian tradition which are not covered in detail in these units. You should also look at passages from the *Reader* for the course[2] when you are directed to them in the units.

The two units are divided into two parts in which you will find Christianity treated in different ways and using different resources. The first part will be more heavily dependent on the essays in the *Encyclopedia* than the second part. Sections 1, 2, 6, 7, 8, 9 and 10 were written by Terry Thomas, and sections 3, 4 and 5 by J.F. Coakley.

The related programme 'Easter worship: the Greek liturgy' on video cassette 1 was filmed in a Greek Orthodox Church in Jerusalem. It gives a rare glimpse of aspects of the Orthodox liturgy which very few even of the Orthodox laity ever see.

Christianity will also be discussed in Unit 16, on audio cassettes 2 and 3, which discuss women in religion and moral decision making, and in the three study guides for this course.

Note that the dates in these units relate to the Christian era, and that therefore the conventional use of 'CE' after the dates has usually been omitted.

1 Zaehner, R.C. (ed.) (1988) *The Hutchinson Encyclopedia of Living Faiths* (4th edn) Century Hutchinson, London (set book); hereafter cited as *Encyclopedia*.

2 Beckerlegge, G. (ed.) (1997) *The World Religions Reader*, Routledge, London (course Reader); hereafter cited as *Reader*.

PART ONE: THE ORIGINS AND HISTORY OF THE CHRISTIAN RELIGION

1 A global perspective

1.1 The Christian religion in today's world

1.1.1 The Christian religion has spread to all continents and penetrated to a greater or lesser extent all the major and most of the minor cultures of the world. It is the largest of the religions in terms of numbers of adherents, though quantifying the adherents of any religion is a notoriously difficult task. The name of the religion derives from the title, the Christ, given to the person who is held to be the founder of the religion, a Jew named Jesus, who was born almost two thousand years ago in Palestine. As might be expected, given such universality, many aspects found in the overall study of religions are to be found in Christianity, though that does not mean that we need to agree with Adolf von Harnack, the Protestant theologian, who said of it, 'Anyone who does not know this religion, knows no religion, and anyone who knows Christianity, together with its history, knows all religion.' The study of Christianity in this course takes its place alongside the study of other major religions of the world.

1.1.2 Christianity may have begun as a Jewish sect in Palestine, but it has become a religion of millions of the inhabitants of the world. It is often classed as a western religion because for many centuries its sphere of influence was Europe and later the Americas. Yet in the past century it has become domiciled in Africa and Asia; especially in the former. In Asia it is still very much a minority religion with a few exceptions, such as South Korea. In Africa there has been a very different story. It is not so much that efforts to indigenize the products of mainstream western churches have succeeded but that Africans themselves have branched out and formed their own churches which are unmistakably African, sometimes showing only faint traces of the religion out of which they have emerged, sometimes showing a great deal of syncretism with the more traditional, pre-Christian, African forms of religion. While there are clear signs that the Christian religion is in recession as a percentage of the population of Europe and, to a lesser extent, North America, it is continuing to grow in Africa, where it is estimated that the number of adherents has been doubling every twelve years since the middle of the nineteenth century. One estimate forecasts that by the end of the twentieth century Africa will have the largest number of adherents of any continent.

1.1.3 In those countries in which Christianity has been dominant it faces many different opportunities and pressures. In eastern Europe and Russia until the early 1990s it had to learn to co-exist with atheistic political domination (*Reader* 2.26, 2.27). In Poland the Roman Catholic Church was the focal point of much social and nationalistic resistance to the Communist regime. In the USA recent years have witnessed the revival of a conservative Protestant Christianity challenging the state on such issues as abortion and the teaching of evolutionary theories of creation in schools. At the same time we have seen Roman Catholics adopting a radically liberal attitude on the same issues and also on issues relating to feminism and clerical celibacy. In Latin America the dominant Roman Catholic Church has been divided into those who wish to maintain the political and social *status quo* and those who advocate various political and social alternatives, including revolution (see *Reader* 2.23). Pope John Paul II, elected to be the head of the Roman Catholic Church in 1978, was active in supporting the challenge to the state in his homeland, Poland, while urging clergy to refrain from political action in Latin America but condemning the poverty and oppression of Latin American countries.

1.1.4 Christians have taken different sides on social issues such as apartheid in South Africa and the future of the welfare state in Britain. Everywhere modernity is a challenge to the Christian religion in respect of the doctrinal bases of the faith and the social and moral teaching which is dependent upon the doctrinal bases. The Christian religion is found across the contemporary world and is an important force in many countries of the south or Third World, not least through its aid programmes. The disparity in the life styles between different groups of Christians, suburban middle class and urban poor, European and American whites and African blacks, is a constant source of debate in such forums as the World Council of Churches.

1.1.5 The basic Gospel of the Christian religion has become a universal message for all races and orders of human beings. Such a universalism has its opportunities and its challenges.

1.2 The Christian religion: uniformity or plurality?

In the units on Hinduism you will be asked to consider whether Hinduism is one religion or many. In *Reader* 4.1, where Wilfred Cantwell Smith discusses Hinduism in terms of its diversity, he refers to a discussion of Islam and Christianity (not included in the *Reader* selection) with the suggestion that these religions too are 'internally diverse'. From the brief look at the recent history of the Christian religion in the foregoing paragraphs, do you think it is a uniform phenomenon or is it, as Smith suggests, internally diverse? It seems that it is certainly internally diverse, perhaps even to the point where it would be more accurate to speak of there being several Christianities, not just one.

Exercise

Turn to the article by Nicholas Zernov in the *Encyclopedia* (p.77, column 2), and read the final paragraph 'As the result ...'. What light does this passage throw on the question of whether Christianity is one religion or several?

Discussion

The author talks of 'two cultures' within a 'common religion'. Yet when you say that you have two distinct cultures, each holding that it alone is the legitimate expression of the common religion, you are not far removed from the notion of two religions. According to Zernov, these two groupings within Christianity have tried to ignore each other and their disunity has damaged the prestige and vitality of the Christian religion. Here we find the notion of unity being elevated to something that safeguards prestige and vitality. The truth is that there is disunity, and we will find that this is a matter of concern for another author in the *Encyclopedia.* But what does disunity amount to? Disunity at the very least means that there is no single church that expresses the wholeness of the Christian religion, and a possible conclusion to be drawn from this is that there is no longer one Christian religion. This feeling is reinforced by Zernov in the *Encyclopedia,* page 83. Read the paragraph that begins: 'It is not easy to define ...'. Here the author suggests that there are at least two groups in the Christian religion who claim their position as the one that is universally valid. Again we meet the question of whether the Christian religion is one religion or many.

And yet we do still talk of *the* Christian religion, and in a way that is not analogous to talking of Hinduism as a single religion. What is it that gives some sort of unity to the Christian religion which is not present in Hinduism? The clue lies in the name given to the religion. Hindu originally meant (for the Muslims who coined the term) the religious practices of those who dwelt beyond the Indus. On the other hand the Christian religion takes its name from the title given to the person who is considered, in some way, to be the founder of the religion, Jesus of Nazareth, who is accepted as the Christ, the anointed one of God. So whatever the appropriate description of the religion, whether it is one religion or many, whether it is internally diverse or not, the one thing that seems to give it some cohesiveness, to give it some unity whatever its internal diversity, is the title given to its founder. The founder was Jesus the Christ, and it is to an examination of his place in the religion that we now turn.

2 Jesus

2.1 Jesus and Christianity

2.1.1 'Christ' (from the Greek) is a word which, by itself, simply means 'anointed'. It thus conveys the same meaning as the 'messiah' of Judaism, but at a very early date it became practically a surname, or alternative name, for Jesus of Nazareth. So when the name 'Christian' was coined – also early, though not during his lifetime – it probably meant no more nor less than 'adherent of Jesus'. This usage illustrates the fact, obvious enough, that what is distinctive about Christianity is the place that it gives to Jesus. Yet it is not so obvious what this place is.

2.1.2 Was Jesus the *founder* of Christianity? The answer to this question is, in an important sense, 'no'. The Christian church does not simply carry on the same message that Jesus preached – the message *of* Jesus – but instead preaches a message *about* Jesus. Modern Christians sometimes recognize this discrepancy and lament it. Why not go back to the primitive undogmatic faith of Jesus' first disciples?

> In simple trust like theirs who heard,
> Beside the Syrian sea
> The gracious calling of the Lord,
> Let us, like them, without a word
> Rise up and follow thee.

Yet although Christians cherish hymns like this one (by J.G. Whittier, 1807–92), such ideas do not add up to Christianity as it has been practised. The first recognizably Christian preaching took place after Jesus' death, and instead of using themes like the 'kingdom of God' which were part of his own language, it was all about the saving value of his death and resurrection. To what extent such a message derives from anything which people knew about Jesus *before* his death is not, on the face of it, easy to say.

2.1.3 How much can we know about Jesus on the basis of the historical sources available? Some scholars hold that the New Testament gospels are so overlaid with theological concerns, or are in other ways so unreliable, that they tell us little of the historical Jesus. If this is a fair estimation, then it becomes necessary to think of Christian faith in a way which does not invest too heavily in 'the historical Jesus'. But no doubt most ordinary Christians do invest their faith in the gospels' pictures of Jesus; and so the idea has grown up that there is a 'gap' between the scholar and the person in the pew. How real this gap is depends on whether an extreme scepticism about the gospels really is justified.

2.2 The gospels

2.2.1 Almost all that is known of Jesus is found in the four 'gospels' of Matthew, Mark, Luke and John in the New Testament. The opinion is sometimes heard that other so-called 'apocryphal' (literally, 'secret') gospels, which differ from the accepted four, might just as easily have been selected for the canon; but most responsible scholars would dismiss the idea. Almost all the apocryphal literature which survives shows signs of dependence on the canonical gospels, or else betrays its late origin in other ways. A very few probably genuine traditions about Jesus show up outside the four gospels, including two or three in the Jewish Mishnah and Talmud, and two in the Jewish historian, Josephus, but put together they would not begin to take the place of the New Testament gospels. So the basis of the 'Jesus tradition' might seem narrow. It looks even narrower when it is realized that Matthew, Mark and Luke, the 'synoptic gospels', are not independent of each other. It is probable that Matthew and Luke both used Mark, as well as another now lost source given the name 'Q' (from the German for 'source'), which was a collection of sayings of Jesus. This view, known as the 'two-document' hypothesis, has some consequences. Stories that appear in Matthew only, or Luke only, may have entered the tradition at the latest stage, and so have to be the most sceptically treated. The best examples are the stories of Jesus' birth and childhood. Another consequence is that none of the three synoptic writers will have been a companion of Jesus. Why not? If the tradition is correct that Mark summarizes the preaching of the apostle Peter in Rome, then it may have been written around the year of his death, about 64 CE; some would put it later. In any case there is a lapse of one generation between Jesus and the emergence of even the first gospel.

2.2.2 The Gospel of John, 'the Fourth Gospel' as it is often styled, has to be considered on its own. This gospel purports to be the work of 'the disciple whom Jesus loved' – an eyewitness, that is, writing at first hand. If the claim is true, then the statements of this gospel deserve to be put on an equal, if not higher, footing than those of the synoptics when it comes to recovering Jesus' life and words. In the nineteenth century such was indeed the consensus, with the result that some of the more tremendous assertions of Jesus, found only in John, like 'I am the bread of life' and 'I and the Father are one', were accepted as genuine. Consequently, some of the Christian message *about* Jesus, that he was God incarnate, seemed to be firmly anchored in the words *of* Jesus. Scholarship has, since then, turned around. Nowadays it is usual to attribute the discourses of Jesus in this gospel to the theological genius of the gospel-writer who, it is said, probably had little or no firsthand information about Jesus anyway. You will notice in your reading of J.G. Davies' article on 'The Early Church' in the *Encyclopedia* that John is never cited in his discussion of Jesus, and when he comes to speak of the Fourth Gospel it is entirely as a work of advanced theology. The present writer thinks this tendency has gone too far. John will be used in some places in our discussion alongside the other gospels.

2.2.3 Besides their distance from Jesus in time, the gospels have another limitation. They are not 'lives of Jesus' in the sense that they set out to answer the kind of questions that a modern person would naturally ask about Jesus. For example, how old was he when he died? Was he a cheerful, or perhaps depressive, person? What sort of family or private life did he have? What did he look like? One could well say that these are religiously important questions, but the gospels hardly touch on them. Broadly, what does absorb their interest is Jesus' death and resurrection. Mark contains sixteen chapters, and the last week of Jesus' life occupies the last six. Secondly, they are concerned with Jesus' *words* – words intended for the benefit of Christian readers, and not primarily for their historical interest. Consequently the gospels often give no information, or give contradictory information, about the original *context* of Jesus' words. For example, according to 'Q' (see section 2.2.1 above), Jesus said, 'Make friends quickly with your accuser, while you are going with him to court, lest your accuser hand you over to the judge, and the judge to the guard, and you be put in prison; truly I say to you, you will never get out until you have paid the last penny.' In Matthew, the saying is part of the 'Sermon on the Mount', and therefore appears as a piece of ethical teaching: do not take your quarrels to the lawcourts. (You may see this in *Reader* 2.3.) But in Luke, although the words are nearly identical, the context shows it to be a parable, or figure of speech. 'Your accuser' is God, and 'you' are the one who must act quickly to avert his unfavourable judgement. Luke is no doubt correct, but the example shows how the interpretation of a particular saying can depend on knowing, as we often do not know, its original setting.

2.2.4 Darkening the critical picture further is the fact that some sayings attributed to Jesus in the gospels seem to have originated with the early church. Examples are too technical to be worked out here, and in the nature of the case they fall short of proof that Jesus could not have said this or that. The easiest cases to see, perhaps, are the interpretations of parables which make them into mysterious allegories (for example, *Mark* 4:13–20) which seems unlikely to have been the original intention. The best general explanation for such 'inauthentic' material in the gospels is that early Christian 'prophets', who we know could speak 'in the name of the Lord', uttered words which then became attached to the historical Jesus, and eventually found their way into the gospels among his recorded sayings. However, given the presence of allegorical interpretation alongside literal interpretation in Jewish sources such as the Mishnah and Talmud, as well as early Christian sources including Paul (*Exodus* 17:6, *1 Corinthians* 10:4), it is quite possible that Jesus offered allegorical interpretation of his own parables.

2.2.5 The drift of the last four paragraphs may seem quite negative. Yet the points raised do not by any means make the 'quest for the historical Jesus' impossible. Two remarks need to be made here. First, given the many subjects on which Christians might have liked to hear words of Jesus – the church and its organization, in particular – it is remarkable how little Jesus is recorded as saying. It must be that the church exercised some restraint in admitting spurious sayings of Jesus into the gospels; and if that is so, we should not expect the authentic material to be swamped by the inauthentic. Secondly, the recognition of what may be inauthentic in the tradition allows what is really authentic to stand out on occasion more clearly. For example, the gospels record that Jesus' disciples were accused of not keeping fasts. Such an attitude would be dissimilar from that of ordinary pious Jews, who fasted regularly, and also from that of Christians who later carried over the Jewish practice. Thus it is difficult to see how this accusation could have been made up if it had no basis in fact. This is an example of the rule that 'dissimilarity indicates authenticity', a powerful tool which allows the scholar to start from those facts and sayings which most certainly attach to Jesus.

You will notice when you read Davies in the *Encyclopedia* that he makes use of the gospels without reference to any of these critical preliminaries. That is because he takes these preliminaries for granted, not because he is uncritical. You should not get the impression from his article that Jesus can be 'read off' from the gospels without very careful attention to these problems of method.

2.3 What did Jesus preach?

2.3.1 The 'kingdom of God' is a prominent theme in the recorded words of Jesus, occurring independently in all the gospel sources (another pointer to authenticity). Our study would be easier if the term had a well-known meaning which Jesus and his listeners understood in common and if Jesus was simply saying something new about it. Unfortunately the phrase is rarely found in the Hebrew Bible, and it is accordingly not obvious that it had a commonly understood meaning. The form in which Jesus presents much of his teaching in the synoptic gospels – the parable– is also distinctive. Students wishing to pursue this point are referred to Drury's (1990) article, which introduces the relevant literature.

Exercise

Read *Encyclopedia*, pages 40 to 44 and especially page 41; look at *Reader* 2.2. Try to write a definition of 'the kingdom of God'.

Discussion

It seems clear that 'kingdom' cannot be thought of simply in terms of a realm or place where God is king. This will work in some of the texts (*Reader* 2.2.1, 2.2.5, 2.2.8) but not in others. Recognizing this, some modern versions of the Bible prefer to translate the Greek word, quite legitimately, as '*reign* of God' – God's sovereignty. Of course, God's sovereignty may be conceived of in various ways: as something that obtains in the world always and everywhere (*Reader* 2.2.2) or specifically in human beings (*Reader* 2.2.8), or which *will* obtain at some glorious future time when evil shall be defeated (*Reader* 2.2.4, 2.2.5, 2.2.6, 2.2.9). The last of these is the one that is probably the most fruitful for the interpretation of the sayings of Jesus, but the exercise is meant to suggest that the term is unspecific and open-ended. A teacher such as Jesus might appropriate it and fill it with his own content.

2.3.2 Many people would say that Jesus spoke of the kingdom of God as something essentially belonging to the future (*Reader* 2.2.3, 2.2.4, 2.2.5). Yet this is only one aspect of the state of affairs. It is too simple a view that Jesus preached a kingdom of God breaking in upon the world in the near future. (If this were the case he was mistaken, and the mistake becomes a problem for Christian belief.) Jesus also saw the kingdom as somehow already present in his own words and especially actions (*Reader* 2.2.6, 2.2.8). Scholars have tried to take account of both these strains by describing Jesus' view of the kingdom of God as 'inaugurated' or 'anticipated'. However there is another consideration. Jesus, apparently deliberately, did not speak plainly about the kingdom. It is typically the subject of parables (*Reader* 2.2.7) designed to engage listeners personally, not to let them form a kind of 'objective' outsider's view of the concept which they could either accept or reject. Thus, 'kingdom of God' stands as a symbol for a transcendent order, but a symbol which seems only to have acquired meaning on Jesus' own lips. Though it is a resonant idea and phrase, and certainly does not disappear from Christian thought, it is not surprising that it was in general displaced by other concepts and themes in the early church.

2.3.3 Some of Jesus' sayings on the kingdom, and many other sayings and stories, involve controversy between him and various Jewish religious authorities. An important question in any assessment of Jesus is, therefore, what was his attitude to his own religious establishment and to Judaism in general? Davies does not take time over it, but it raises other questions about the development of Christianity as a religion separate from Judaism, and it has an obvious interest in the context of this course.

2.3.4 In the unit on Judaism it was mentioned that the Pharisees were 'democratizing' scholars whose aim 'was to teach the people how to embody the teachings of God in their daily lives', and whose work saw the Jewish religion through the destruction of the Temple in 70 CE. A statement like this, as the unit author recognizes, means that the gospels' picture of the Pharisees as exclusionist and trivializers of the Torah must be in some degree wrong. This is possible: many scholars explain the gospels' polemic against the Pharisees as the church's reading-back into Jesus' day its own attacks on the synagogue a generation or more later. In this case, Jesus did not, in reality, differ fundamentally from the Pharisees; perhaps he only said things (such as, 'Let the dead bury their dead', *Matthew* 8:22) which shocked rabbis who had more official responsibilities. But it is also possible that the Pharisees in Jesus' day were not the popular leaders that they became later. Almost all of what the Mishnah records about them pertains to ritual purity, and specifically to regulations about food which – it may be argued – were beyond the means of ordinary people to keep. If that is so, the gospels' picture may not be so far wrong. (The question is very controversial, and depends at least as much on the interpretation of rabbinic texts as on the New Testament.)

2.3.5 Jesus' attitude to Judaism may be investigated from a different angle by examining his pronouncements and actions which seem to involve a critique of the Torah itself. Here too there are difficulties. Consider for example the saying in *Mark* 7:15: 'there is nothing outside a man which by going into him can defile him; but the things which come out of a man are what defile him.' At first sight the judgement of the New Testament theologian Ernst Käsemann seems correct: 'When Jesus refuses to agree that man contracts defilement from external sources, he is abandoning the foundation principle on which the whole Jewish cultus was based.' That is, Jesus made a plain assertion that the Torah was in this respect superseded. Yet, there are reasons for hesitation. The saying comes in the middle of a paragraph in which the debate is over the washing of hands. This excites suspicion that it originally belonged in some other context, with all the uncertainty that implies about what it might have meant there. More generally, if Jesus expressed himself so clearly as a critic of the Torah, it may be wondered why the fact was not a greater scandal than it was, and why the church later had such trouble deciding whether to insist that its non-Jewish converts should be brought within the Jewish religion. On the whole it does not seem conceivable that Jesus attacked the Torah directly. The radical tendency of some of his statements comes, no doubt, from his conviction of who he was: 'lord even of the sabbath' (*Mark* 2:28). This is not to say the sabbath-law is overturned, only that the demands of the kingdom of God can take precedence over it. On the other hand, with some justification Christians took Jesus' words to be, by their implication, an assertion that some other ideal had replaced the law. All this lies behind what Paul says, that 'Christ is the end of the law' (*Romans* 10:4).

2.4 Jesus Christ, Son of God

2.4.1 There would be a link with the Christian preaching about Jesus if this preaching took over titles which Jesus had applied to himself. It is noticeable, however, that in the gospels Jesus appears reticent about claiming or making up any titles for himself at all. (This is less so in John than in the others, but it is still the case.) The exception is the term 'the Son of man', which appears in many sayings. Christians sometimes explain this title as one that Jesus used in order to emphasize his humanity in contradistinction to 'Son of God'; but this distinction is never made in the gospels. In fact its sense is obscure. It *may* have been some sort of 'messianic' title known in Judaism (Davies, in *Encyclopedia*, p.42, seems to hold this view, but others, pointing to the fact that 'son of man' is an Aramaic idiom simply meaning 'man', disagree). (On Jewish understanding of the 'Messiah' see Units 1–2, section 4.3.1.) The point is controversial, but need not detain us here: what is significant is precisely that the early Christians did *not* preach that 'Jesus is the Son of man'.

2.4.2 According to the Acts of the Apostles, the very earliest Christian preaching described Jesus as 'the Christ'. This is a remarkable fact if indeed Jesus did not claim the title during his lifetime (as Davies says, *Encyclopedia*, p.42). Several explanations are possible. The Gospel of Mark supposes that he *did* accept the title, only enjoining his disciples to keep his messiahship secret until after the resurrection; but this is almost certainly Mark's own idea and not based on genuine tradition. Another explanation is that whatever Jesus' attitude to the title may have been, it stuck to him. 'When the Christ appears, will he do more signs than this man has done?' say the people (*John* 7:31). And perhaps Jesus even invited it. According to Luke, in his first synagogue sermon Jesus applied the prophecy of Isaiah to himself: 'The Spirit of the Lord is upon me, because he has *anointed* me to preach good news to the poor' (*Luke* 4:18). No doubt the Messiah was, in most people's minds, a nationalistic champion after the model of the ancient Israelite kings (*Encyclopedia,* p.35), but the wider meaning of 'anointed one' was not forgotten.

2.4.3 The other title which the early church favoured for Jesus was 'Son of God'. At first glance, this title appears to say something about the way Jesus was 'begotten'. Taken at its maximum of literalness, and combined with the story of Jesus' virgin birth, it could be understood to imply that with Jesus God took the place of a human father – and one may hear this opinion put with varying degrees of sophistication by many Christians. But in fact the origin of the term has nothing to do with Jesus' birth. It may be traced to Jesus' characteristic address to God as 'Father'. That Jesus called God 'Father' (Aramaic *Abba*) is one of the most certainly known characteristics of his words. It is dissimilar from the Jewish practice, which was to use more distant addresses, like 'Our Father, Our King'. To be sure, Jesus taught his followers to think in the same way, and to begin their prayers, '*Father*, hallowed be thy name' (*Luke* 11:2). Accordingly, later Christian writers such as Paul and John speak in different ways about *all* Christians being 'sons of God' or 'children of God'. But there were other sayings of Jesus which practically reserved the title to himself. Davies mentions a few of these (*Encyclopedia,* p.44), drawing the conclusion that Jesus claimed a unique 'filial' relationship to God. Another example is the parable of the 'wicked tenants' (*Mark* 12:1–9 and parallels) in which, after other agents are ill-treated, the owner of the vineyard sends his most trusted representative, his *son*, to collect the rent on his property. Whether Jesus really was speaking of himself or not, it was inevitable that the church should interpret the parable in that way: Jesus was so far superior to the prophets in his ability to represent God that only the metaphor of *son*ship would adequately describe him. So this christological title, apparently so 'high', has a good foothold in the words of Jesus.

2.5 The death of Jesus

2.5.1 The discontinuity between Jesus and the Christian message about Jesus seems to be at its sharpest here. Typically later Christian creeds attach some positive theological value to the death of Jesus: he was 'crucified *also for us*' (Nicene Creed, *Reader* 2.10); he 'suffered *for our salvation*' (Athanasian Creed, *Reader* 2.11). The fact that they do not spell out its significance is only because in the early centuries the point was not controversial and did not demand any more precise definition. On the other hand, looked at as an event of history, Jesus' untimely death by crucifixion was to Christians obviously a tragedy. A frequent human response to tragedy is to search for someone or something to *blame*.

2.5.2 Taking the question of 'blame' first: the tendency of Christian tradition has unfortunately been to exaggerate the responsibility of the Jewish people, either the population of Jerusalem as a whole, or the religious leaders, for the condemnation of Jesus. This tendency may be observed at its clearest in the addition which Matthew makes to Mark's narrative: Pilate, the Roman governor, washes his hands and says, 'I am innocent of this man's blood'; and the people answer, 'His blood be on us and on our children!' (*Matthew* 27:24–5). Some scholars likewise doubt whether Jesus was ever formally brought to trial before the Jewish Sanhedrin, as Mark (though not John) relates. In fact, some go so far as to argue that Jesus' real offence was one of sedition against the Roman government of Judaea. His punishment was the one usually meted out to terrorists, and it is not necessary on this showing to assign the Jews more than a very small part in the story.

Certainly the anti-Jewish tendency in the gospels is to be admitted; but it is jumping too far to conclude that the issue lay between Jesus and the Romans, and not the religious authorities of Judaism. For one thing, in spite of ingenious attempts to find them, there are almost no positive indications in the gospels that Jesus was interested in violence against the Roman government. At most, this may have been a course which attracted him early in his career but which he then renounced. For another (to recall section 2.3.4–2.3.5), it seemed that Jesus' words represented a threat to the party of the Pharisees, if not more generally to the place of the Torah in the Jewish religion. Certainly he was seen as an unsettling influence by the Temple establishment. John records the fears of the high priest: 'If we let him go on thus, everyone will believe him, and the Romans will come and destroy both our holy place and our nation' (*John* 11:48). This seems a plausible statement. Jesus' activities were subversive of *religious* authority, but in so far as this authority co-operated with the Roman government, he might be seen as a threat to the political order of the country. Exactly how the religious leaders framed a charge against Jesus which stood up in the Roman governor's court is not completely clear; but it is apparent that both Jews and Romans had a part in the proceedings.

2.5.3 Whatever the historical circumstances of Jesus' death, Christian reflection had some basis for a positive view of it. First of all there was the bare fact that Jesus accepted, and did not try to escape, this death. He is recorded as predicting it; and even if not all the details of these predictions are authentic, it seems probable he at least said such words as 'the Son of man *must* suffer many things' (*Mark* 8:31). It is debatable what 'necessity' Jesus was referring to – some allusion to the so-called Suffering Servant of God in the book of *Isaiah* is likely – but at least it would put his death into some kind of theological context. More than this, it appears Jesus himself attached a value to his death. 'The Son of man came not to be served but to serve and to give up his life *as a ransom for many'* (*Mark* 10:45). At his last Passover meal with his disciples, Jesus interpreted the wine as his blood, 'which is poured out *for many'* (*Mark* 14:24). The value of vicarious suffering was understood in Judaism, and there seems no reason to deny that Jesus spoke in such terms about his own death.

2.5.4 These data were the raw material for Christian doctrine. The earliest form which survives is probably the simple statement which Paul says he 'received', that 'Christ died for our sins' (*1 Corinthians* 15:3). It is interesting to compare what three different New Testament authors make of the idea.

(a) Luke clearly minimizes it. Even the two sayings just quoted from Mark have no clear parallels in his gospel. Other evidence of his point of view comes from the speeches which he records in his other composition, the *Acts of the Apostles*. (*Encyclopedia*, pp.44–6, takes these speeches to represent accurately the earliest Christian preaching, but in this respect they seem to be eccentric.) The speakers in *Acts* do not go beyond saying that Jesus was 'delivered up according to the definite plan and foreknowledge of God ... But God raised him up' (*Acts* 2:23–4). In other words, the death of Jesus is significant only in so far as it is reversed by his resurrection.

(b) Paul, by contrast, takes the death of Jesus as of the first importance in the whole process of salvation by which God reconciled the world to himself, 'making peace by the blood of his cross' (*Colossians* 1:20) – though, as Davies suggests (*Encyclopedia,* p.48), this is part of a conception of redemption which takes in the resurrection at the same time.

(c) The writer to the Hebrews (not Paul, according to scholars) (see *Encyclopedia,* p.50, and *Reader* 2.5.2), again differently, expounds the death of Christ as a sacrifice more acceptable to God than those sacrifices of the ancient Jewish cult. The New Testament gives the impression that reflection on the death of Jesus was open to different estimations and metaphors. The concept of the Atonement, as such reflection is broadly called, has accordingly always been a comparatively open field, and not one where precise official definitions have been made by the churches (*Encyclopedia,* p.67).

2.6 The Resurrection

2.6.1 That God raised Jesus from the dead 'on the third day' is the other focal point of Christian belief. By its nature, however, it is more problematic than belief in the death of Christ which, whatever its interpretation, was a plain fact. No one claimed to see the resurrection happen. What the New Testament records is that (a) Jesus' tomb was found to be empty on the third morning, and (b) Jesus appeared to various of his followers on and after this same day. Of these two traditions, the empty tomb sometimes figures larger in modern Christian apologetic, as if the resurrection might be 'proved' if all the other explanations for it could be ruled out. But this line of argument is never very compelling, and in any case no one would have come to believe that Jesus had risen from the dead on this basis alone. If we are to speak of any event or experience causing the belief in Jesus' resurrection, it must be the appearances of Jesus to his followers.

Exercise

In *Reader* 2.4 are printed the four main texts in the New Testament which describe or list the appearances of Jesus after his death. From reading 2.4.1, 2.4.2, 2.4.3 and 2.4.4, try to draw some conclusions about the tradition as a whole and how it developed.

Discussion

In general the gospels preserve two traditions about Jesus' appearances, one centred in Galilee (Matthew) and the other in Jerusalem (Luke). John sides with Luke, though the last chapter of his gospel, obviously added later, is a Galilean story. Paul's list of resurrection appearances (*Reader* 2.4.5) overlaps the gospels' with Peter and the twelve disciples, but is otherwise different. In particular it includes larger groups – 'all the apostles' and 'five hundred brethren' – and Paul himself. It is an unavoidable conclusion that the texts do not agree with one another. This fact is sometimes taken as a sign of the unreliability of them all, but it is equally possible to see it as indicating a very primitive core (perhaps only the bare appearances themselves) which has been developed in different ways. Paul's inclusion of himself in his own list is also striking. He is presumably referring to his experience on the Damascus road (*Acts* 9:3–9), though to the modern reader this does not look like a 'resurrection appearance'. All these facts suggest that in the earliest times the conception of an 'appearance' must have been elastic, and all kinds of claims to appearances must have been entertained. As Paul suggests, such claims may have been made especially by those seeking to establish their qualifications to authority in the church. They may have gone on for a long period: only in the late gospel of Luke are matters neatened up by the inclusion of an 'ascension' after forty days which terminated them.

2.6.2 Within the New Testament, the theology of the resurrection was variously expressed, for example as God's vindication of Jesus by raising him to his right hand in heaven (*Reader* 2.4.7), or as an anticipation of the general resurrection of believers (*Reader* 2.4.6). The words of Paul, 'If Christ has not been raised, your faith is futile' (*I Corinthians* 15:17) are often quoted to show that belief in Jesus' resurrection is the central doctrine of Christianity. Yet it can occupy a greater or lesser place in actual Christian thinking and piety. Consider the statement of the mid-twentieth-century theologian Rudolf Bultmann that 'faith in the resurrection is really the same thing as faith in the saving efficacy of the cross' (Bartsch, 1972, p.41). The Christian gospel is thus a message about the *death* of Christ which is only confirmed by God in the resurrection. Very broadly, in western churches reflection on the death of Christ probably preponderates over reflection on his resurrection. The greater part which it has in hymn writing is nicely shown by the fact that the *Reader* contains three hymns on the former (2.14.1, 2.14.2 and 2.14.3) and only one on the latter (2.14.4); and hymns specifically on the resurrection are mostly reserved for the Easter season. The point is made from the Orthodox side by Zernov in *Encyclopedia*, page 86.

3 Orthodoxy and heresy

3.1 Heresy

3.1.1 Christianity, more than some other religions, has traditionally been concerned with defining correct and incorrect belief. This may be because Christianity has no other basis of self-definition to fall back on (membership of an ethnic group for example). It may also be a necessary concern in a large institution with some measure of central control and with temporal power. However valid these explanations may be, the categories of 'orthodoxy' and 'heresy' were established early in Christian history, and it is in terms of conflict between the two that Christian doctrine is often studied. Undoubtedly controversy was of the first importance to the development of doctrine. But the use of words like 'heresy' can be dangerous, as the following exercise will show.

Exercise

Consider the following statement:

> Heresies always represent the erection into a system of undue or partial emphasis on a particular point of view ... For orthodox theology heresy is, therefore, at once an opportunity for progress and a danger of one-sidedness. Whenever an erroneous emphasis or statement is made, the organism of the Church stiffens into concentrated resistance, with the result that since error is always partial, dogmatic truth runs the risk of appearing partial as well.
>
> (Congar, 1939, p.29)

With what definition of 'heresy' does the author operate? (Answer this briefly.) How might a historian find this definition inadequate to work with?

Discussion

In the quotation, 'heresy' means simply 'false doctrine' – or, according to the official Roman Catholic definition – the 'denial or doubt of any doctrine of the Catholic faith'. Speaking dogmatically and with suitable ideas of what is 'Catholic', one may find this satisfactory; but it is another question whether it can be used with reference to real historical controversies. The difficulty arises from the fact that 'heresy' has always been defeated, or at least has not prevailed over 'orthodoxy'. On the dogmatic definition of heresy we would be committed to a 'triumphalist' view that truth has always defeated error. Now this *may* in fact be the case, as many Christian scholars would argue. Alternatively, a more cynical view is possible. 'History,' it might be said, 'is written by the winners. Right or wrong, they called themselves "orthodox" and their opponents "heretics".' There is no way to decide between these two views in advance: the arguments have to be set out for each individual controversy. In the meantime, if the words 'heresy' and 'orthodoxy' are to be saved, they must be understood to have some neutral meaning. One possibility is to define heresy as 'doctrine which was rejected by a consensus of Christians at a particular time'. But since the word is so suggestive of 'error', the most careful practice is probably to avoid it altogether in discussing the history of doctrine.

3.1.2 The opposite of 'heretical' is 'catholic', and this word shares the same ambiguity. According to the classical definition of Vincent of Lerins (fifth century), catholic doctrine is *quod ubique, quod semper, quod ab omnibus creditum est* ('what has been believed everywhere, always, and by all'). This corresponds to the 'consensus' definition of heresy just mentioned, except that it surely goes too far. It suggests that there was, as the New Testament puts it, 'the faith once for all delivered to the saints' (*Jude* 9). No doubt it is possible to speak of a 'deposit of faith' in this sense, but it will have included only the barest preaching of Jesus' death and resurrection. We have already seen how in the New Testament there was no single doctrine of the Atonement (the reconciliation of God and humanity through Christ); and the Trinity and the incarnation (sections 3.2 and 3.3 below) furnish even better examples of what was undefined in early Christianity. So, for example, when the so-called Athanasian Creed (*Reader* 2.11) expounds 'the Catholic Faith' at length and with great technical precision, it must be using the word in a dogmatic rather than a historical way. Even so – that is, taking 'Catholic Faith' to mean 'correct faith' – this creed is something of an embarrassment. Even to unscholarly Christians, it has seemed wrong to define orthodox belief in so narrow a way. The Anglican prayerbook prescribes the recital of this creed on various occasions in church, but the practice is very rarely followed nowadays.

3.2 The Trinity

3.2.1 The doctrine that the one God exists in three 'persons' – Father, Son and Holy Spirit – is (together with the incarnation) the most distinctive of all Christian tenets. It is shared by all traditional denominations and was, for example, written into the 1961 statement of the basis of the World Council of Churches.

> The World Council of Churches is a fellowship of churches which confess the Lord Jesus Christ as God and Saviour according to the Scriptures and therefore seek to fulfil their common calling to the glory of the one God, Father, Son and Holy Spirit.

It is well known that this conception is not found in the New Testament, although there are some suggestive forms of words such as *Matthew* 28:19, Jesus' command to baptize 'in the name of the Father, the Son and the Holy Spirit'. The doctrine of the Trinity reached a definitive form in the fourth century; the culminating point in the development of the early church's doctrine.

Davies' discussion in *Encyclopedia*, pages 55 to 59, may be read as a clear account of how this climax was reached. You should notice in your reading that the course of development was not dictated by inner logic alone. Such logic by itself might more naturally have led to a 'binitarian' (belief in God in two modes – transcendent and immanent) doctrine. That is, on the basis of experience, God might have been spoken of as one person transcendent (say, the 'Father') and one person active in the world (say, the 'Word'). This seems to be implied by some Christian writers of the second and third centuries, although the same writers seem to be restrained by the *three*-fold formulas which they knew from the New Testament. Or again, trinitarian doctrine was at many points a response to 'heresies', Sabellianism and Arianism (denying the full divinity of Christ) in particular. This fact is responsible for some particular features of the orthodox understanding of the Trinity. For example, according to the 'Cappadocian Fathers', there is no distinction among the three persons in what they *do*; all have a part in creation, redemption, sanctification and inspiration. This was an important argument in defence of Nicene orthodoxy. To deny it might be to suggest that the three persons were not 'of one substance'. Yet if it is so, it follows that the doctrine of the Trinity cannot be based in any obvious way on the Christian experience of God – a rather unnatural result. These two examples at least raise the question whether the doctrine of the Trinity was a necessary conclusion, or whether in different circumstances some other formula might have emerged. (See further Wiles, 1976, pp.1–17.)

3.2.2 Although the formal terms of the doctrine of the Trinity are (with one exception) the same in all Christian denominations, there is a characteristic difference between eastern and western churches in the way these words are expounded. Eastern Christian thought starts in general with the evident distinction of persons in the Trinity and tries to understand their mysterious unity as one 'God'. As an analogy, 'We may be confronted by many who individually share in human nature, such as Peter, James, and John, yet the "man" in them is one' (Gregory of Nyssa, *On Not Three Gods*). Such analogies make the doctrine vivid and easy to grasp, but it runs the risk of sounding 'tritheistic'. Western thought on the other hand, starts with the unity of the godhead and tries to understand its three-ness. One way has been to define the persons in their relations *to each other.* This is probably 'safer', but the price to be paid is that the doctrine becomes abstract and religiously insignificant. It may be said that most western Christians, beyond repeating the creed, hear and think little about the Trinity except in liturgical churches on the one Sunday of the year devoted to it, Trinity Sunday.

The other difference between East and West may be seen by comparing the Nicene Creed as printed on page 76 of *Encyclopedia* with that in *Reader* 2.10. The latter is the western version, asserting that the Holy Spirit proceeds from the Father '*and the Son'* (Latin, *filioque*), a fifth century addition to the creed. In its defence, Catholic theologians have held that there must be some defined relationship, such as 'procession', between the Son and Spirit, if the two persons are not to collapse into one; whereas the Orthodox hold that the Father is the focus of unity in the godhead and the only source of the other two persons. The *filioque* has been the ground of extraordinary controversy (*Encyclopedia*, pp.79–80), though nowadays it seems obvious that, in view of the mysteriousness of the whole concept of the Trinity, neither side could, or even should, expect to enforce its view on the other.

3.3 Christology and incarnation

3.3.1 Broadly, 'christology' takes in all the language used in answering the question 'Who was Jesus?'. The basic Christian answer to that question, and the common property of all traditional Christian denominations, is that Jesus was 'God incarnate'. So the subject of christology in the first place is the doctrine of the incarnation. More narrowly, 'christology' can also mean the particular line of thought which *presupposes* that Jesus was God incarnate, and then tries to define how he could be both God and man. Thus church historians speak of the 'christological controversy' which blew up after the settlement of Nicaea and which was resolved – as far as most churches are concerned – at the Council of Chalcedon in 451.

3.3.2 The doctrine of the incarnation, like that of the Trinity, was not there at the very beginning of the history of the church. It is worth looking again at Davies' summary of the 'primitive preaching' (*Encyclopedia,* p.45) to convince yourself that it contained nothing about Jesus being God, or anything more than a man, until after his resurrection. It is equally certain that by the time of the Nicene Creed, the doctrine had reached its full development. Look at this creed in *Reader* 2.10. In general, it contains two layers of christology, representing the two significant developments of the primitive preaching. The top layer, so to speak, is that which is directed against Arius: that is, that the Son was 'very God of very God', 'begotten, not made' and 'of one substance with the Father'. The Arians had maintained a different view of Christ, that he was a 'creature' who belonged to a lower order of being than God himself: he could be called 'God', but only as a 'courtesy title'. His status was *achieved* by his perfect obedience to the Father. The church ultimately rejected this view, chiefly it seems because the notion of salvation which it entailed was weak in comparison to the 'orthodox' doctrine. This, expounded powerfully by Athanasius, was that salvation meant 'deification', which only God himself could confer. However, the pros and cons of the Arian controversy are hard to interpret sympathetically: the whole debate assumed, as modern people do not, that there was some category in between 'man' and 'God' to which Jesus *might* have belonged. A livelier subject of scholarly interest has been the deeper layer in the creed: that Jesus 'came down from heaven ... and was made man' – that is, that he had an existence with the Father before his incarnation as a human being. The New Testament writers, Paul and John in particular, are commonly thought to hold that Jesus was pre-existent. Davies, for example (*Encyclopedia,* p.49), points to the evidence of *Philippians* 2:5–11 (text in *Reader* 2.4.7). Yet if we take 'emptied himself' here to be a description of what Jesus did in submitting to death on the cross, rather than in coming to be born, it is not so obvious that pre-existence is in Paul's mind. Likewise in *John* 6:42, some of the language which seems to mark off Jesus as a pre-existent divine being, like 'come down from heaven', is not far removed from what can be said of anyone, that he might be 'born from above' (*John* 3.7). The discussion of texts is too complicated to pursue here (see Dunn, 1980), but it does appear that the New Testament is 'softer' and more nuanced on the conception of pre-existence than the later creeds which built upon it and used its words.

3.3.3 Davies' discussion of the christological controversy of the fifth and sixth centuries (*Encyclopedia,* pp.60–4) is admirable. It only needs to be added for the purposes of this course that the divisions caused by this controversy still exist. From the point of view of the Latin West and much of the Greek East, Chalcedon did 'establish', as Davies says, the norm of christological belief that Christ was two natures in one hypostasis. But this was not so in Egypt, Syria or Armenia, where monophysite views prevailed. The christological controversy was ended not by argument but by the Islamic conquest of these regions. The Muslim rulers were indifferent to whether the Christian church was united or not, and so the political pressure to come to a settlement was removed. Further to the East, in the former Persian empire now also under Islam, the church had yet a different and strongly anti-monophysite tradition, and in the seventh century it adopted an official christology which spoke of 'two natures and *two* hypostases'. All these 'non-Chalcedonian' churches (whose history in between then and now must be passed over) survive. The Syrian Orthodox, Coptic Orthodox, Ethiopian Orthodox and Armenian Orthodox churches are collectively known as the Oriental Orthodox churches (they usually deprecate the name 'monophysite'). Since the 1960s they have held conferences together with the Greek Orthodox and Roman Catholic churches, aiming at theological reconciliation. This has been surprisingly easy. For example, in 1971 part of an agreed statement between Catholics and Oriental Orthodox read as follows:

> We believe that our Lord and Saviour, Jesus Christ, is God the Son Incarnate; perfect in his divinity and perfect in his humanity. His divinity was not separated from his humanity for a single moment, not for the twinkling of an eye. His humanity is one with his divinity without commixtion, without confusion, without division, without separation.

> We in our common faith in the one Lord Jesus Christ, regard his mystery inexhaustible and ineffable and for the human mind never fully comprehensible or expressible.

This is an example of how christological agreements can be reached if the traditional formulas, which are entrenched and contentious, are avoided, and if it is agreed to leave open whether any particular person was a heretic or not. The 'Church of the East', the old church of Persia (less satisfactorily called 'Assyrian' or 'Nestorian'), is now a very small body, mostly dispersed in Europe, America and India, and consequently more theologically isolated, though the same comments would broadly apply to its doctrinal position.

3.4 The East–West schism

3.4.1 The word 'schism' (Greek *schisma*, 'tear, rent') is preferred to describe the historic division between the Christian 'East' and 'West', 'Orthodox' and 'Catholics'. Formally, 'schism' is distinct from 'heresy' in that no matter of doctrine is involved in the break in relations. Yet in practice the distinction is not always maintained. As Jerome said (end of fourth century), 'There is no schism which does not invent some heresy for itself.' Thus, under certain circumstances, as in the eleventh century when feelings ran high, the differences between the two bodies were seen as touching the catholic faith itself and accusations of heresy were exchanged. The state of affairs is set out by Zernov in *Encyclopedia*, pages 78 to 79. You should notice particularly his analysis of the underlying reasons for the schism. It was a long and gradual process; the date 1054 when the communion was formally broken off marks only one episode, and not even the last one, in it. In modern ecumenical times, the language of 'heresy' is rarely used between great churches, and even the language of 'schism' is moderated. The second Vatican Council declared that other Christian communions were in 'a certain, albeit imperfect, communion with the Catholic Church'.

3.4.2 Read Zernov's sketch of the modern Orthodox church in *Encyclopedia*, pages 83 to 93. It should be said that, masterly as this is, it is written from the inside and presents a picture which is in many respects idealized. To Catholic and Protestant eyes, this tendency is clearest in the section on 'The authority of the Church'. The Orthodox concept, in which this authority resides in 'the whole body of the faithful', appears at first sight deeper than doctrines of infallibility of the Pope or the Bible. But it means in practice, as Zernov says, that to be authoritative decisions on doctrine must be made and accepted by *all* the Orthodox. Furthermore, according to the Orthodox view, only decisions of seven 'ecumenical councils' actually meet this criterion to qualify as authoritative. The last of these (which vindicated the use of icons) took place in the year 787. A critical study of these councils is in some tension with the heavy weight of authority which they are made to bear; but the problem is not just one of history. Orthodox theology, though it did not stop in 787, is inherently conservative, appealing as it seems exclusively to ancient authorities and dismissive of new departures and formulas which – or so more liberal church people of other denominations would hold – are needed if the faith is to be expressed in a changing world. The idea that women might be ordained to priesthood, for example, remains practically unthinkable among many Orthodox, although some Orthodox women are discussing issues of ordination.

4 Religious life: the outlines

4.1 Baptism

4.1.1 From the very earliest times baptism has been the characteristic action of Christian initiation. At his first sermon, the listeners asked Peter 'What shall we do?' to which he answered, 'Repent and *be baptized*, every one of you, in the name of Jesus Christ' (*Acts* 2:37–8 in *Reader* 2.6.3). Now why Peter should enjoin baptism is not at all clear as the account stands, and indeed the origin of the practice is left surprisingly obscure in the New Testament writings. Matthew makes it a command of the risen Jesus to baptize, but it cannot have been as simple as that. His disciples must have been prepared for it somehow (*Matthew* 28:19 in *Reader* 2.6.1). The only pre-Easter baptism which the gospels mention is the one administered by John the Baptist. Jesus underwent this, and even baptized others for a time (though this latter fact is mentioned only in *John*). This was a baptism 'for repentance', a point in common with Christian baptism. Yet John the Baptist disappears from the gospels well before the end, and it seems unlikely that Christian baptism can simply be a continuation of his practice. A more likely explanation is that Christians took over the Jewish practice of baptizing proselytes. This custom is not well known, partly because it does not figure largely in modern Jewish life. Study of the rabbinic literature, however, throws up enough correspondences, especially between the structure of the Jewish and Christian rituals, to make it very probable as the parent of the Christian rite.

4.1.2 However, it seems that the significance of baptism differs substantially between early Christianity and the Judaism of the period. In Judaism, circumcision was the theologically more significant rite of initiation; the convert's baptism was viewed as part of the beginning of his or her new life, but beyond that the texts are too weak to build on. This fact itself is significant, however. It looks as if in the Christian church the actual *practice* of baptism came first, its interpretation being elaborated later. Consequently this interpretation was open to variation: for example, baptism might be a dying with Christ, a rebirth, or the washing away of sins. Davies documents these and other ideas on pages 67 to 68 of *Encyclopedia*. One of the interpretations he mentions deserves further comment. Baptism is associated by several New Testament writers with the reception of the Holy Spirit. Luke, however, sometimes operates with a different conception. In one of his narratives, the people of Samaria are evangelized, but not by an apostle. Peter and John then 'came down and prayed for them that they might receive the Holy Spirit; for it had not fallen on any of them, but they had only been baptized in the name of the Lord Jesus. Then they laid their hands on them and they received the Holy Spirit' (*Acts* 8:15–17). This text has been the chief authority for a separate rite of 'confirmation' in which after baptism the Christian is understood to receive the Spirit in a new or fuller way. It is now, however, administered differently in different churches. Among the Orthodox it follows baptism immediately in the same service. In some other churches, individuals are confirmed by the bishop after a course of instruction by the local priest.

Exercise

The practice of all ancient churches of baptizing newborn babies has been controversial since the sixteenth-century Reformation. Two questions have been at issue: (a) is it likely to have been practised in the earliest times? and

(b) is it agreeable with a proper understanding of baptism? Read *Encyclopedia*, pages 68 to 69, and the texts in *Reader* 2.6 and 2.7, and try to answer these questions, or at least say why they are so difficult.

Discussion

The majority of scholars (including Davies) do not find evidence in the New Testament that the earliest church baptized babies. At best, a 'household' which was baptized might have included children, though even then not necessarily very young ones; and Jesus' commandment not to 'forbid' children might, or might not, have been taken by the early church to be significant in a baptismal context. The quotation from Origen (in the 230s or 240s CE) to the effect that infant baptism was a tradition from the apostles should not be given too much weight: the point is precisely that he *needed* to argue this because there were those in his time who did not accept the custom (see *Reader* 2.7). It is on the whole best to see the rise of the institution alongside the developing ideas of 'original sin' in the third to fifth centuries. If sin was inherited, then the newborn baby stood in need of the antidote of baptism from the very beginning of life. The argument seen here from Origen and later elaborated by Augustine amounts to one theology of baptism which could justify an answer 'yes' to the second question, though it is not one that modern liturgies exploit. Instead, the main idea they express is that a baby is welcomed into the 'Lord's family'. On the other side, those who reject the baptism of babies usually appeal to the theology of baptism which emphasizes repentance and commitment such as only an older person can express. The trouble is that both these views have their own logic and can find support in the New Testament texts. As we said above, the institution of baptism came first, and different meanings, some of them contradictory, were laid onto it. Put another way: baptism, and specifically infant baptism, is a symbol, and one cannot normally say that a symbol is right or wrong, only that it has, or has not, power for those who use it. Such judgements are always subjective. Feminist theologians argue that infant baptism developed as a way for the male priesthood to confer 'life' – replacing the blood of physical birth with the water of baptism.

4.2 The eucharist

4.2.1 The other basic Christian rite is the eucharist, also known as 'Lord's Supper', 'Mass' or 'Holy Communion'. For each Christian, baptism is a single event, but the eucharist is repeated regularly. In Orthodox, Catholic and usually Anglican parishes it is the main Sunday service each week. In many religious communities it is celebrated daily. Protestant churches usually observe it once a month as an appendix to the ordinary Sunday service, though there is some variety in practice here. The worshipper's particular part in the eucharistic service is to partake of consecrated bread and wine (or in the usual Roman Catholic practice, only of the bread). In early times, Christians may have made their individual communions only once a year, and infrequent communion, four times a year or less, is still the Orthodox practice. In the West, all the faithful usually communicate at each eucharist.

4.2.2 Traditional eucharistic liturgies hark back to the Last Supper of Jesus with his disciples, quoting his words over the bread and wine as the 'words of institution' of the rite (see *Encyclopedia*, p.69). This fact seems to answer the question of the origin of the eucharist straight away. Yet it is likely that some elements of the early eucharist derive rather from other meals shared by Jesus and his followers, especially after the resurrection.

Luke relates how two disciples first failed to recognize the risen Jesus; then 'When he was at a table with them he took the bread and blessed and broke it and gave it to them. And their eyes were opened and they recognized him' (*Luke* 24:30–1). A story like this suggests that Jesus' *presence* with his disciples was especially remembered in the church's 'breaking of bread'. Some scholars go so far as to suppose that the later eucharist was a combination of two different observances, one deriving from the Last Supper at which bread and wine were taken and interpreted, and the other a kind of fellowship meal at which Jesus' presence was celebrated and his return anticipated. This theory may be pressing the evidence too hard, but it is a useful analysis to keep in mind when reading Davies' generalized presentation of the meaning of the eucharist (*Encyclopedia*, pp.70–1). In any case, the Last Supper themes, in particular that of sacrifice, soon took over, and are the dominant ideas in all traditional liturgies, East and West. In the West, the 'liturgical movement' in the last two generations has been responsible for some changes. Responses like 'The Lord is here', 'His Spirit is with us', as well as a more demonstrative 'peace' exchanged among members of the congregation, are elements in modern liturgies that try to recapture some of the primitive fellowship themes in the eucharist which were later crowded out.

4.2.3 The Byzantine and Latin eucharists have in common the nature of representing Christ's sacrifice. But as East and West were progressively estranged, the two liturgies also developed characteristic differences. The programme 'Easter worship: the Greek liturgy' on video cassette 1 shows the most important of these. The first is that the Orthodox faithful do not see much of the ritual, which goes on beyond the iconostasis. This is a somewhat different way of arriving at the sense of awe and mystery which the Latin Mass traditionally cultivates by means of the elevated altar, and open space between priest and people. Equally noticeable is the richness of ornament in the eastern rite. Vestments, incense, icons, three ministers and music, are all essential. There is nothing to correspond to the Catholic 'low mass'. This is because, as the programme says, the liturgy is 'a momentary joining with the worship of the saints and angels', and so the splendour of the liturgy reflects that of heaven. (Whether this has a deeper explanation in the particular Orthodox belief that 'matter is spirit-bearing', as Zernov says in *Encyclopedia*, pp.84–5, may perhaps be left open.)

Another difference between East and West is the treatment of the eucharistic elements. The high point of the western eucharist is the consecration, or elevation of the consecrated 'host' (wafer). At this definite and solemn point the elements begin to be treated as the body and blood of Christ. In the eastern liturgy, the moment at which the elements become the body and blood of Christ is less important, or even undefined. The ritual of the prothesis, seen in the programme, calls for the priest to stab the bread with a lance, as if re-enacting the piercing of Jesus' body. Likewise the 'great entrance', at which the elements are brought from the prothesis table to the altar, is probably the climax of the service for the congregation, although again the elements are not yet consecrated. Indeed, it is not laid down whether the important moment comes at the words 'This is my body ...', or at the prayer known as the *epiclesis* which calls for the Holy Spirit to be sent down to the elements to make them Christ's body and blood. The difference is typical of the analytical way of looking at the liturgy in the West, and the less precise way in which the Orthodox see the meaning conveyed by the whole liturgy.

4.3 Church order and ministry

4.3.1 The oldest officers in the church are of two kinds. First were the 'charismatic' leaders, so called because they appear in a discussion of spiritual gifts (*charismata*) in *1 Corinthians* 12: 'God has appointed in the church first apostles, second prophets, third teachers, then workers of miracles, then healers, helpers, administrators, speakers in various kinds of tongues.' Little is known about churches who operated solely under this sort of leadership. Perhaps Paul's congregation at Corinth was the only one that ever did. Paul's letters to them demonstrate how unsatisfactory it must have been. When another group of 'apostles' came to Corinth and began to preach (as it seems) in different terms from Paul's, Paul called them 'false apostles' (*2 Corinthians* 11:13). Yet he had no means of proving his accusation, precisely because the claim to a 'charismatic' gift is by its nature not something that is easy to test. In other words, charismatic leadership was inadequate to deal with disagreements or conflicting claims to authority.

The other kind of officers in the earliest churches, and the only ones to survive officially into the second century, were locally appointed 'presbyters' and 'deacons'. Unlike the office of 'apostle', which had a considerable theology attached to it, these officers were basically servants of the local congregation and administrators. A 'presbyter' was, literally, an 'older man': churches, just like synagogues, were managed by 'elders'. Deacons (literally, 'servants') held the lower office, whose duties were probably taken up chiefly with distributing alms.

Exercise

You may notice that the office of 'bishop' has not been mentioned. The word (Greek *episkopos*) does occur in the New Testament, but always as a synonym for 'presbyter'. In other words, the three-level hierarchy, bishop–presbyter–deacon, cannot be found in the earliest sources. It shows up first in the letters of Ignatius, Bishop of Antioch in *c.*100 CE. A part of one of these letters along with an extract from Irenaeus's *Against Heresies* (end of the second century) are printed in *Reader* 2.8 and 2.9. From reading these consider how the office of 'bishop' may have come about.

Discussion

Irenaeus and Ignatius give somewhat different impressions. Irenaeus, concerned to refute the teachings of the 'gnostics', uses the argument that orthodox teaching was handed down from the apostles along a succession of bishops to the present day. The inference from his words would be that the office of bishop was created for doctrinal reasons: to pass on the orthodox faith. No doubt this inference is partly true; but the idea of a one-to-one succession from the apostles is a later construction. As we said above, the idea that there was a chain of *single* bishops is not supported by the earliest sources. Ignatius's letters are more revealing. In the church of Smyrna (and others) there was apparently a schism between two parties. But if the bishop could assert his sole authority (it was Ignatius's idea to supply him with a letter to strengthen his hand), the parties would have to come together under him. However the system of single bishops got started – no doubt by one of the presbyters assuming a chairmanship – it had its justification in terms of harmony and unity in the local congregation.

4.3.2 In the hierarchy bishop–presbyter–deacon, it only remained for 'presbyter' to become 'priest' to reach what essentially obtains today in episcopally ordered churches. There are extra grades on top (metropolitan, patriarch) and on the bottom (subdeacon, reader) which need not be considered here. The English word 'priest' is in fact derived from 'presbyter' but the idea of priesthood did not at first attach to the office in anything like the Jewish sense of 'one who offers sacrifice'. The bishop who celebrated the eucharist, which was seen in one way or another as representing Christ's sacrifice, would have been closer to that model. But from the second century on, bishops were not multiplied in country areas, and presbyters became the usual celebrants of the eucharist. When, still later, men were ordained to the office of presbyter independently of any duties in a local church, the idea was confirmed that ordination conferred priestly status on an *individual.* Such ideas, along with the conception of the eucharist as a sacrifice, were repudiated at the Reformation, and now Protestant churches do not call their pastors 'priests'. (In Anglican churches, the title has come back into use since the Oxford Movement in the nineteenth century; see *Encyclopedia,* pp.112–3, for a brief account of Anglo-Catholicism and the Oxford Movement.)

4.4 Ascetics and monks

4.4.1 Even a brief sketch of the basic Christian institutions of ancient times has to mention monasticism, the life of Christian devotion lived apart from the world. By the sixth century monasteries were flourishing in all Christian lands and in many places were the principal Christian institution. This flowering of monasticism was quite rapid, since its history only begins in the late third century. At this time it emerges, seemingly independently, in two different places, Egypt and Mesopotamia. In the latter place we find Christian hermits taking to the desert and living lives of often extreme austerity and self-punishment. They ate and slept as little as possible; some rejected any manufactured shelter or clothing; some are even said to have provoked animals to attack them. When they died their bodies were sometimes not found for years. Such a radically life-denying ideal could, just possibly, be derived from the words of Jesus, but it seems so strange as to require some other religious input. Probably this input was from Manicheism, a religion which held a much more negative view of the physical world and was more thoroughgoing in its asceticism. In any case, the Mesopotamian style of monasticism did not spread widely. It is the Egyptian movement which was the ultimate ancestor of all others.

The first to go out into the Egyptian desert was Antony, about 285. His pioneering life, and the widely read biography of him, probably written by Athanasius, led many others to follow. Antony is said to have responded to a sermon on Jesus' words in *Matthew* 19:21, 'If you would be perfect, sell what you possess and give to the poor, and you will have treasure in heaven.' This story raises the question again whether the monastic impulse does legitimately derive from Jesus. On the one hand, there are a number of sayings which lend themselves to such a conclusion: Jesus' words in this saying, for example, could be taken to refer to a goal of 'perfection' which was not for everyone but only a few who could renounce the world. On the other hand, it is clear that Jesus himself was thought by some to be 'a glutton and a drunkard' (*Matthew* 11:19), certainly not an ascetic; and he specifically wished his disciples not to go 'out of the world' (*John* 17:15). In any case it is reasonable to look for other impulses to monasticism which might have operated in Egypt at this time. Before 313 the persecution of the church by the Roman Empire may have been a factor. But the end of persecution and the beginning of official favour with Constantine from 313 may also have led some into the desert: a favoured, increasingly wealthy church perceived to be in collusion with the authorities may have seemed at odds with the radical, alternative kingdom suggested in parts of Jesus' teaching. There may also have been non-religious reasons for becoming a monk – for example, to escape the tax collector.

4.4.2 From a movement of individuals monasticism soon became something more organized and disciplined. Some of this organization derived from Antony himself. He attracted disciples in numbers, and although preferring solitude he found himself making rules for those who built their cells in clusters around his. This kind of arrangement, in which hermits grouped together, living mostly independently but sharing worship at some times, spread especially to Palestine. A monastery of Mar Saba, southeast of Jerusalem, still exists. Meanwhile a more powerful movement was at work in Egypt. After a period as a hermit, Pachomius (*d.c.*349) founded a community in which the monks lived three to a cell, ate, worked, and said daily prayers together. As the *Life of Pachomius* says, 'theirs indeed was a *koinobion*' (Greek *koinos*, 'common' + *bios*, 'life') – hence the name 'coenobitic' for this, the dominant form of monasticism today. The ideal was not ascetical, and although the monks' life was simple and hard, self-chastisement or extra prayer or fasting by individuals was discouraged. Pachomius eventually presided over eleven monasteries, of which two were for women. His organizational model was taken up by Basil (329–79), reckoned the patriarch of Greek and Russian Orthodox monasticism; and it also made its way to the West. There its structure was further worked out in the 'Rule of St Benedict', composed in the second quarter of the sixth century at Monte Cassino in Italy. The regime provides for an elected abbot who rules for life. The occupation of the monks is principally the daily services of prayer (the 'Divine Office'), to which are added reading and work. The monks hold all property in common. The rule is otherwise not strongly ascetical.

4.4.3 Even before the end of this period of evolution, monasticism was a powerful institution. Some of this power was exercised in doctrinal controversies. Cyril and his successors as Patriarchs of Alexandria doubtless owed some of their power to the army of monks loyal, and even fanatical, in the cause of the Alexandrian christology. And on the other side the *Acoemetae* ('sleepless ones' – they sang psalms in shifts all day and night) were the champions of Chalcedon. In other circumstances the monastic establishment formed a kind of alternative to the ordinary ('secular') hierarchy. In early Irish Christianity, for example, monasteries took the place of parish churches. Finally, the importance of monasticism in the wider intellectual history of the world, in preserving classical learning and books through the Middle Ages, is well known. It applies to Greek monasteries – specifically in Islamic times to those on Mount Athos, the 'Holy Mountain' in Greece – as well as to the Benedictine monasteries of western Europe, which through the Dark Ages often formed the only kind of social organization in western Europe which transcended local ethnic boundaries. This institutional structure was to emerge in the Middle Ages as a central pillar of society in western Europe, in what was later to be known as 'Christendom'.

The next section moves on to the Protestant Reformation of the late fifteenth and sixteenth centuries, but those wishing to gain an insight into the theology and spirituality of the medieval period are referred to Davis' article 'Christianity: St Thomas and medieval theology' in *Encyclopedia* (pp.94–100), and to the extract from Julian of Norwich in *Reader* 2.19. Aquinas' synthesis of Augustine and Aristotle and the mysticism represented by Julian laid the foundations for the intellectual and mystical traditions respectively of contemporary Catholicism.

5 The Christian religion in the modern world

5.0.1 In this section we will look very briefly at the history of the Christian religion from the sixteenth to the twentieth century. You have already learned something of the great schism which divided East and West in section 4.4, and the end of the previous section pointed you to reading on the medieval period. Here, however, we are more concerned with the second great division in the history of the Christian religion, which led to a division of the western church into the Roman Catholic Church and the various Protestant churches.

In studying the events of the Protestant Reformation and the subsequent Roman Catholic reaction it is generally accepted that the events were the result of developments which took place in the preceding centuries. There is some debate, however, concerning the balance of influence of one development against another.

Exercise

Please read *Encyclopedia*, page 129, column 2 'The Reformation ...' as far as page 130, column 2 '... from 1552–1563'. Try to evaluate the argument as it is outlined by Corbishley. He makes a number of statements about the state of the Christian religion in Europe before the Reformation but he isolates one factor as outweighing all others. Can you spot that factor and evaluate what weight he gives it? Then identify the factors that are given lighter weight.

Discussion

The factor that is given most weight by Corbishley is the political one. It 'far' outweighs 'the purely religious factors'. He then goes on to list a number of states where the rulers 'conspired to defeat the Church's attempts to preserve religious unity'. This last remark is interesting in itself. It assumes that there was a unity in the church which was broken in the sixteenth century. A few lines before he says that the church had survived 'the Avignon exile and the Great Schism'. The 'Avignon exile' refers to a period when the papacy was resident in Avignon. When the residency was restored to Rome in 1377, a further two rival Popes persisted at Avignon until 1408, and this was known as the 'Great Schism'. This embarrassment to the papacy was overcome, but you will remember from section 3.4 that there was an earlier Great Schism, that between 'western Catholic' and 'eastern Orthodox' Christianity, and that has persisted until this day. So what Corbishley describes as 'the Church', the unity of which he was concerned had been lost at the Reformation, was in fact already part of a disunited Christian religion.

Turning to politics, it is right to point to the emerging power of the modern nation state and the resistance of such states to papal interference in internal matters, but note that out of five states mentioned by Corbishley, in only two of them was there any significant political influence which led to the emergence of Protestantism. The 'independent spirit of the German princes' did produce one form of Reformation, and 'the autocratic temper of Henry VIII' produced another. But whether this political situation was more important than religious factors needs to be examined carefully.

On the religious side it is clear that a number of developments had been taking place for some time. One might ask, for instance, why it was necessary for the late medieval scholars of the church to write their massive treatises in which the appeal to reason was brought in as the servant of theology. One answer is that there were signs of dissent from the accepted orthodoxy of the church, and Anselm in the eleventh century and Thomas Aquinas in the thirteenth century were trying to shore up the bulwarks of orthodoxy. Thus when new challenges to that orthodoxy began to appear towards the end of the fifteenth and the beginning of the sixteenth century it was apparent that some massive change was on the way. Therefore, one of the roots of Reformation was the backlash against the orthodoxy of the middle ages and was brought to the surface by the new, or rediscovered learning, which goes under the name of the Renaissance. Those who engaged in this radicalism did not intend to revolt against Rome – indeed some of them remained within Rome or died for their loyalty to Rome. Among the most famous of the former was Erasmus of Rotterdam, and among the latter Sir Thomas More, who said of the orthodox theologians, the schoolmen, 'I might as soon obtain bodily nourishment by milking a he-goat into a sieve as spiritual nourishment by reading the schoolmen.' Part of this radicalism was a new awareness of the Bible and a more critical approach to the text of the New Testament as ancient manuscripts were uncovered.

The more this frame of mind took hold, the more also was the revulsion against some of the devotions that grew up in the Middle Ages. The devotions were related to an increasing number of localized cults surrounding statues that bled, or bleeding Hosts (the consecrated bread kept near the altar and adored), or statues of the Virgin Mary that rolled their eyes. Erasmus and like-minded persons were contemptuous of and angry with these manifestations of popular piety. They considered that such practices were not merely conducive to incredulity and irrationality but a dangerous threat to 'true' religion. The income generated by these cults was in addition to income already accruing from the sale of ecclesiastical livings and of indulgences. These indulgences were based on the belief that the sinner suffered physically in purgatory on account of sins committed in life. The punishment in purgatory could be alleviated by the prayers of saints, through the merits of the sacrifice of Christ and through other means, such requests for remission to be accompanied by the gift of money. The practice reached scandalous proportions just before the Reformation. The matter came to a head under Pope Leo X, who promulgated the sale of indulgences as church dogma and accepted some of the proceeds of the sales for the rebuilding of St Peter's Basilica in Rome. This act became a direct cause of the Reformation.

It has been said that the prevailing religious attitude of western Christianity in the Middle Ages was the strong sense of sin, and obsession with the means of removing the effects of sin. The answer of the church was to intensify its image, through its various offices, as the sole purveyor of grace – God's unmerited help that enables believers to live a Christian life. In particular, attendance at Mass was the main source of grace. The consecration of the bread and wine and the elevation of the bread, the Host, was the central act of piety and the effective transmission of grace according to medieval spirituality. It was not necessary for the faithful to receive the bread and the wine. They were expected to be only witnesses of the miracle of the altar. The effect was that the receipt of grace became virtually a mechanical event though accompanied by much piety. For the vast majority of the faithful such a mechanical view of grace sufficed and brought great comfort. This was especially true if you were wealthy enough to be able to pay for special masses. For others it was not acceptable, and indeed was seen as a scandal in which the efficacy of belief in the saving grace of salvation through Jesus Christ was replaced by the manipulation of the church through its ritual structures.

One of the ironic facts of the pre-Reformation period was that reform was not called for on account of irreligion, which might be deduced from an account of the abuses perpetrated by the clergy. The period before the Reformation was highly religious. It saw the emergence of the Pieta, the portrayal of the dead Christ in the arms of his Mother, as a symbol of devotion. It also saw the introduction of devotions such as the Stations of the Cross (a series of prayers and meditations on the stages in the story of Jesus' crucifixion) and the Angelus (a devotional exercise repeated three times a day commemorating the incarnation). The fifteenth century had seen true religion as understood by the church pursued with great vigour in the Spanish Inquisition. Indeed, it has been argued that the Reformation occurred not because of irreligion but because Europe had become very religious; so religious that abuses would not be tolerated. On the other hand, attempts by successive Popes to reform the church had ended in failure. It appeared that if reform was to be achieved then it would happen in spite of the church. Minor reforms were carried out, but only through the power of secular authority. By all accounts Henry VIII was not merely a person of 'autocratic temper' but also exceedingly pious.

So, while it is true that the Reformation cannot be explained on the grounds of religious factors alone, and it is true that politics did play an important part in the process, it should also be realized that political power was closely allied to the strong desire for religious reforms, of a kind the Popes seemed unable to bring about.

5.1 The Protestant Reformations

In the *Encyclopedia* you will find that the title of the first section of Kent's article 'Christianity: Protestantism' is 'The principles of the Reformation'. Corbishley also refers to the event in the singular but it is noticeable that in his article he goes on to talk about what happened in the Roman Catholic Church as a response to the event, and the way in which the church instituted its own reforms partly was a result of what the Protestant reformers had been saying and doing. There are some who refer to the events of the period as Reformation and Counter-Reformation, but there are others who refer to the events as the Protestant and Catholic Reformations.

The following historical details are not given in the articles by Kent and Corbishley. The Protestant Reformation can be divided into at least four distinct divisions. These are the German Lutheran, the Swiss, the so-called Radical, and the English Reformations. I will deal with them in that order. The main element of the Catholic Reformation was the Council of Trent: for further information on this see Corbishley's account on pages 130 to 132 of the *Encyclopedia*.

5.1.1 The German Reformation

Martin Luther (1483–1546)

Martin Luther was a monk of the order of Augustinian Friars and Professor of Scripture in the University of Wittenberg, Germany. The events surrounding his life can be seen as the outcome of a number of factors. There was the religious attitude of the order he belonged to, one of rather 'exaggerated pessimism'. Then there was his own rather melancholy but also passionate nature. In addition there was his massive erudition as a philosopher and interpreter of scripture. In his late twenties he began to entertain severe doubts about his ability to attain moral perfection in spite of the diligent ways in which he carried out his religious duties as a priest and religious supplicant. The doctrine of the church proclaimed that diligence in confession, the celebration of the Mass and the reciting of the daily offices, would guarantee salvation on account of the grace flowing through these rituals. But in spite of rigorous discipline in these matters Luther could never feel confident of salvation because he felt no relief from the awareness of sin and the burden of guilt which arose as a consequence.

In 1512 or 1513 Luther claimed to have had a climactic religious experience while he was reading his Bible. The experience was some kind of disclosure which convinced him that the essence of the Christian gospel was that a person is 'justified by faith and not by works of the Law'. Corbishley defines justification as 'the process whereby the sinner is restored to the favour of God, his virtues developed, his salvation achieved' (*Encyclopedia*, p.138). What this experience resulted in is discussed in the *Encyclopedia* passages I want you to read in a moment.

The crisis in Luther's life reached a crucial point when an indulgences 'pedlar', John Tetzel, appeared making extravagant claims for his wares. The result was the posting by Luther of the notorious Ninety-five Theses on the door of the castle church in Wittenberg on 13 October 1517. The Theses directly attacked the sale of indulgences but indirectly the power and authority of the Pope. They were publicized throughout Germany in a short time. The Pope had to act. Luther was made to answer to charges of heresy. In a series of disputations and in the face of a trial *in absentia* in Rome, Luther refused to recant and eventually was led to declare that neither the Pope nor the General Councils of the Church were infallible. There followed a number of publications in which he called for secular authorities to take over the reform of the church, which attacked church practice in withholding communion from the faithful, attacked church dogma relating to the doctrine of transubstantiation as applied to the eucharist, reduced the number of sacraments to two, baptism and the eucharist, as the only ones prescribed by Jesus, and finally proclaimed the freedom of the faithful person from the obligation of performing good works. In 1520 the Pope moved decisively against Luther in a papal bull, censuring forty-one of his theses as heretical, ordering his books to be burned and himself to be put under a ban unless he recanted. Luther's reply was to burn the bull and a number of Catholic books. He was excommunicated on 3 January 1521.

In the years that followed the foundations of a new form of the Christian religion were laid. Luther wrote forms of worship which conformed to his main religious beliefs. He wrote commentaries on certain portions of scripture in the same vein. The hymns he wrote during this period have become classics in hymnology, and he translated the Bible into German, thereby making it accessible to the German people. Some of his initial supporters divided from him, many of them becoming more radical in their reforms. His support for the authorities in their war with the peasants has been severely criticized and his whole approach to the alliance between church and state, with the state being given major powers in the control of religion, has brought him severe critics and enemies over the intervening centuries.

5.1.2 The Swiss Reformations

Ulrich Zwingli (1484–1531)

Although the Reformation in Switzerland is more commonly associated with John Calvin, there was a reform movement that took place in Zurich before Calvin arrived in the country. The first reforms took place under the influence of Ulrich Zwingli. He was initially influenced by Erasmus but was mainly affected by his devotion to the study of the Bible. The reform in Zurich began with Zwingli's lectures on the New Testament while he was a minister in the city. In his sermons he attacked ideas of purgatory, the invocation of saints and the institution of monasteries. In 1522 he published his first Reformation tract in which he advocated freedom from the control of the Pope and bishops. In a disputation with a representative of the Pope he won wide support and proclaimed the supremacy of scripture while rejecting the authority of the Pope, the sacrifice of the Mass and clerical celibacy. Eventually he clashed with Luther over the interpretation of the action of the eucharist. Zwingli maintained that in the rite any reference to the body and blood of Christ was merely memorial, rejecting any 'real presence' (see below) of Christ in the action. He also found himself in contention with Anabaptists (see 5.1.3). He was more radical than Luther but not as radical as those who are commonly considered to be the 'Radical' reformers.

John (Jean) Calvin (1509–64)

French by birth, Calvin is known for his work as a reformer in Geneva. His first experience of Protestant reform came while he still lived in France, where he had given up an early intention to follow a priestly career and was studying law. Like Luther, he had an intense religious experience which convinced him that he had a vocation to restore the church to its original purity. This advocacy of Protestant principles led to his being forced to flee France and settle for a time in Basle, Switzerland. In 1536 he published what has always been regarded as his major work, *The Institutes of the Christian Religion.* In the same year he was persuaded to settle in Geneva and be jointly responsible for the leadership of the Reformation there. In a short time he had published his *Articles of Church Regime.* All citizens of Geneva were to be subject to the regime which controlled admission to the Lord's Supper and personal belief. Those who did not submit were to be exiled. All the citizens had accepted the oath by 1538. The severe application of the regime and Calvin's refusal to conform to the stronger regime at Berne led to his own expulsion. Over the next few years in Strasburg he formed close friendships with other reformers such as Martin Bucer and Philipp Melanchthon.

Calvin was invited back to Geneva in 1541 and spent the next fourteen years establishing a theocratic state there. A strong ecclesiastical form of government was conceived which ruled not only the church but the city as well. Legislation covered all manner of religious offences and prohibited gaiety in the form of dancing and games. Not only were people excommunicated after trial but even tortured and executed. The most famous victim was Michael Servetus, who denied both the doctrine of the Trinity and the divinity of Christ and who narrowly escaped the Catholic Inquisition. In Geneva he was found guilty of heresy and burned at the stake. From 1555 onward Calvin was virtually the supreme dictator of Geneva, carrying on with ruthless logic his ideas on theology and church order. His most remembered article of belief was that of double predestination, that is not only does God predestine some to everlasting glory but he also predestines others to everlasting perdition. A strong doctrine of predestination is common to many forms of the Christian religion, and indeed religions other than Christianity. It arises from belief in the absolute supremacy and foreknowledge of God. The Reformation tradition which arose out of the doctrines of Calvin still exercises influence in a wide area of Protestantism. The Presbyterian form of the Christian religion, which includes the Church of Scotland, traces its roots back to Geneva.

5.1.3 The radical reformers

The reforms we have just been looking at and the English Reformation we shall look at below are often referred to as the 'Magisterial Reformation', meaning that they were carried out in agreement with the secular authorities in each case. Those reforms that were carried out independently of legal authority are in contrast referred to as 'Radical'. Reference has already been made to the Anabaptists. The name means those who 're-baptized'. They did not belong to any particular country, but their main concentrations were in Switzerland, south Germany and Holland. There were a few in England from 1534 onwards. The most well-known groups were the Swiss Brethren, Moravians, Hutterites (after their leader Jacob Hutter), and the Mennonites.

Their main doctrinal feature was that baptism could only be administered on the basis of a personal confession of belief, hence the exclusion of infant baptism and the re-baptism of those who had been previously baptized as infants. They also tended to be pacifist and to advocate forms of non-violent resistance to state authority, and hence to reject government by magistrates, to hold property in common ownership and to reject any centralized form of church government, vesting authority rather in the individual congregation. This type of Christianity has resulted in denominations of a Baptist, Congregationalist or Independent kind in Britain and elsewhere, especially in the USA.

There is one other main grouping which is listed under the 'Radicals' and they are the 'anti-Trinitarians', or Unitarians, that is, those who reject belief in the divinity of Christ.

5.1.4 The English Reformation

In the English Reformation there was no gradual, unbroken progression from one stage to another. Events that took place under Henry VIII, such as the suppression of the monasteries and the reduction in holy days and popular devotions, and the crucial event of Henry's divorce which offended Rome, were, strictly speaking, more to do with stabilizing dynastic succession and keeping out foreign interference, as well as filling badly drained coffers, than with the desire for religious reform. However, there were Lutheran supporters in the University of Cambridge, some of whom later became Protestant bishops. Henry himself, while acting against the Pope and achieving supremacy over the church in England, remained Catholic in his religious persuasion. An earlier attack on Luther's teaching had earned him the title 'Defender of the Faith' conferred on him by Pope Leo X in 1521. As late as 1539 Henry reasserted his Catholicity in the 'Six Articles' and demonstrated his repudiation of Protestantism in his marriage to Catherine Howard.

Henry had allowed the use of the Bible in English which was, in effect, a reforming act. His son Edward was a boy when he succeeded to the throne and was dominated by his leading noblemen. Thomas Cranmer, the powerful Archbishop of Canterbury who had eased the path of Henry in his dispute with Rome, was freed to introduce Protestant ideas. This he did through the publication of his *Book of Homilies*, the two Books of Common Prayer of 1549 and 1552, described as 'the greatest monument to his genius', and the Forty-Two Articles of Religion (1553) which, though never enforced because of the succession of the Catholic Mary in the same year, became the basis for the Thirty-Nine Articles of Religion which have persisted to this day. It is claimed that between 1549 and 1553, under the rule of the Protector, the Duke of Northumberland, England admitted as much reform as any German or Swiss city had done.

Under Queen Mary Tudor the Protestant religion was proscribed and England returned to the sphere of Rome. A number of leading churchmen, having at first been dealt with leniently, were later burnt as heretics. They included Thomas Cranmer. On her death she was succeeded by Elizabeth I and for a time the church was both Catholic and Protestant. The population was predominantly Catholic in their sympathies but there was a growing party of Protestants who eventually gained the ascendancy with the appointment of Matthew Parker as Archbishop of Canterbury. The Prayer Book of 1552 was reissued in 1559 with modifications designed to reduce offence to Catholics. Elizabeth's sympathies were Lutheran in respect of the relations between church and state. Parker's sympathies lay with the Calvinists but with a strong sense of the middle way. The Thirty-Nine Articles of Religion which were accepted under Parker were more Calvinistic than Elizabeth would have liked, but she needed the support of the Protestant party to strengthen her throne. In 1570 Elizabeth was excommunicated by the Pope. England became a clearly Protestant country and a leader of European Protestantism, but with a Protestant church which retained a fair measure of Catholic order alongside Lutheran polity and Calvinistic doctrine.

5.1.5 The Encyclopedia articles

Exercise

Please now read the *Encyclopedia*, pages 101 to 107 and 128 to 133 (top of column 1). Note the salient points made by each author and compare the way in which they view the Reformation overall and their own side in the events. Kent, you will find, roams forward in history to make his arguments concerning the Protestant Reformation, while Corbishley sticks more closely to the immediate events, and especially to the Council of Trent. Be aware of the possibility of bias in the accounts and try to identify statements which contradict each other in describing the situation.

Discussion

John Kent centres the cause of the Protestant Reformation almost exclusively on Luther's personal crisis and religious experience and what we might call Luther's radical view of the operation of the grace of God. Thereafter the thrust of Kent's account is to establish that the Reformation was not a negative event nor an extreme event to offset anti-Protestant criticisms. The negative aspect is held to relate to the very name of the reformation – Protestant. The name comes from the proceedings of the Diet of Speyer (1529) when a Catholic group tried to withdraw rights from Lutherans in certain Catholic districts. Certain princes and cities made a declaration 'protesting' freedom of conscience and the rights of minorities. The protest, it is therefore held, was a positive act not a negative one. Kent calls as witnesses Richard Hooker, the archetypal moderate in the Church of England of the sixteenth century, and E.B. Pusey, a good witness since he was a leader of the catholicizing party in the Church of England in the nineteenth century. The one testifies to the reasonableness of holding a strong doctrine of justification by faith and not by works; the other testifies to the continuing errors of Rome and the reasonableness of the position of the Church of England as a reformed but catholic church. Kent claims that Luther (and Calvin for that matter), kept the essentials of primitive Christianity and only discarded those elements which were later, unnecessary accretions. In detail: by having a strong doctrine of justification by faith, Luther did not intend hope and charity (the other cardinal virtues) and good works to be neglected. The restoration of the social aspects of the eucharist was positively good – something that Rome, according to Kent, is belatedly accepting in the twentieth century. In addition the Reformers did not set aside the ancient creeds nor exalt private judgement in matters of doctrine. Authority was one of the aspects of Catholicism which the Reformers kept. Protestant doctrine kept the most important aspects of traditional doctrine, except among the most radical. Continuity of patterns of worship suffered far more than patterns of dogma. The pattern over the whole of Protestantism was not uniform. The Church of England kept many of the forms and appurtenances of pre-Reformation worship as did some areas of European Lutheranism.

As might be expected, and this is where some bias might be at work, Kent sees the Protestant Reformation as a wholly beneficial event. Not only is there no questioning of what Corbishley refers to as disunity, but there is commendation of the 'earnestness of the leading Reformers' in allowing 'separate ecclesiastical bodies to come into existence wherever the secular power was willing to accept and foster them' (p.102).

Corbishley, by contrast, persists in putting high value on the unity of 'the Church', in spite of the fact that the body represents only one part of the Christian religion. Interesting also is his use of the term 'Christendom' in the context. Henceforward Christendom is to be divided. The term is seldom used nowadays but was used to define the Christian religion as some kind of global community. We have already discussed the division of the religion before the Protestant Reformation. An Eastern Orthodox leader was led to say that Pope Leo IX, the Pope at the centre of the Great Schism, was the first Protestant.

Corbishley gives us the essence of what happened as a result of the Council of Trent in the long quotation on page 131. It is a summary of the Catholic Reformation. You will see that Kent is right when he says that in no way did Catholic reform go far enough to meet the demands of the reformers who ended up as Protestants. Corbishley sets the parameters of reform in his statement that 'the Church' must be conservative and progressive. By conservative he means not changing anything that had been established by earlier general councils, or doctrines that were considered to advance Catholic understanding of the faith. Doctrine could change, that is, the church could be progressive in Corbishley's terms, except that what he sees as progress is often seen by Protestants as further regression.

This is so especially in respect of doctrines associated with the Virgin Mary. Kent, in quoting Pusey with approbation, points out that Pusey was speaking before the First Vatican Council of 1869–70 which established the dogmatic status of the Immaculate Conception, and well before the Bodily Assumption of Mary was promulgated as a dogma in 1950. Protestants, even in today's ecumenical climate, view these decisions as anything but progressive. You may have noticed that the dogma of the Immaculate Conception actually has its roots partly in the account of the Tridentine (that is, of the Council of Trent) teaching on Original Sin. The human race, according to Trent, was subject to Original Sin and therefore in need of baptism which was effective in removing all taint of guilt of sin. Corbishley adds that the Council explicitly excluded Mary from the scope of the universality of Original Sin. The force of this is to remove the taint of sin one further stage from Jesus, who was made 'to be sin who knew no sin, so that in him we might become the righteousness of God' (*2 Corinthians* 5:21). The force of the dogma of the Immaculate Conception is to claim that Mary herself was born free of the taint of sin. The same force is at work in the stories of the birth of Jesus.

Likewise the reaffirmation of the doctrine of transubstantiation in respect of the eucharist would appear to the Protestant Reformers as regression. The doctrine of 'transubstantiation' is an attempt to explain how the risen Christ is actually present in the eucharist in the bread and wine, which according to the gospel narratives of the 'Last Supper' were to be his body and blood. It is the issue of the 'Real Presence' or not of Christ in the sacrament. Simply described, a sacrament is 'an outward and visible sign of an inward and spiritual grace'. Outwardly in the eucharist the visible signs are the bread and wine. Inwardly the spiritual grace is the presence of, or the efficacy of, the body and blood of Christ, symbolizing salvation through the death of Christ in the elements of bread and wine. There are a number of possible interpretations of this sacrament. Four common ones are:

(a) the bread and wine are actually the body and blood of Christ;

(b) the spiritual presence of the body and blood exists along with the bread and wine;

(c) the body and blood are somehow spiritually present in the blessing, giving and receiving of the bread and wine, i.e. in the action of the rite, the body and blood being in heaven and not present;

(d) the action is merely commemorative.

These four stances cover the range of Catholic and Protestant views.

The first of these can be interpreted in more than one way. A common way of interpreting it in the Anglican tradition is to say that it is a mystery to be accepted but not analysed. It is summed up in a rhyme allegedly spun by Elizabeth I herself.

> Twas God the Word who spake it,
> He took the Bread and brake it,
> And what the Word doth make it,
> That I believe and take it.

Another way of interpreting it is by the doctrine of transubstantiation. This doctrine demands a certain philosophical view of matter. According to this view matter is made up of two parts, substance and accidents. The substance of matter is its intrinsic quality. Bread has the substance of breadness which may be recognizable by the smell, taste and texture of the bread, but these qualities are its accidents. The accidents may change, the bread may become mouldy, its taste and texture may change, but its substance remains the substance of breadness. Nothing, according to this philosophy, can take away its breadness. In the eucharist, however, according to this doctrine, a miracle occurs: the bread when it is consecrated retains its accidents (that is, taste, smell and textures), but its substance is changed from that of bread to that of the body of Christ. The same applies to the wine, hence transubstantiation. This means, if we accept the doctrine, that the bread is no longer really bread but the body of Christ. The doctrine is extended to the point where the 'body' as with a normal body contains also the 'blood', so it becomes unnecessary to receive the communion in both kinds, another distinction between Protestant and Catholic eucharistic practice and theology. The bread or 'body' received in the form of a wafer is not to be chewed according to some Catholic teaching as this would lead to the release of 'blood'. In more recent times many Catholic teachers have tried to modify this teaching but it was rejected a long time ago by the Protestants. In this respect the official teaching of the Church of England on the subject makes it very clearly a Protestant church.

Article XXVIII of the Thirty-Nine Articles of Religion states that the doctrine of transubstantiation is rejected on the grounds that it 'overthroweth the nature of a sacrament'. It is the only eucharistic doctrine that is dealt with in any way in the Book of Common Prayer. The reasoning behind the statement has to do with the basic sacramental principle that matter can be a vehicle of divine power. But as a vehicle it retains its materiality otherwise the notion of sacramentality is undermined or 'overthrown'. The miracle is not in the transformation of matter but in the use that God makes of matter. If the matter is held to be transformed into something else, say into the divine itself, then that can become the basis of idolatry as, indeed, some Protestants would argue it has been in the adoration of the Host on the basis of the doctrine of transubstantiation. Idolatry occurs when the object which is accepted as a vehicle of the divine is perceived as the divine itself. Idolatry, in essence, irrespective of the form of the symbol, occurs when the symbol of the ultimate is itself given ultimacy.

Finally let us consider what Corbishley has to say about the operation of grace in the light of human sin. The Council of Trent agreed that 'natural virtue and the fulfilment of the Law of Moses could not, of themselves, give man supernatural life, which could come through Christ alone', but this was not sufficient in itself, for moral observance was also needed. At this point it is interesting to note the difference between Kent's view of Luther and Corbishley's. Kent argues that Luther knew he ran the risk of the kind of accusation levelled by Corbishley on page 131, column 2, and dealt with again on page 132, columns 1–2. The Council appealed to scripture, in this case the words of Jesus that one must 'keep the commandments'. Corbishley goes on to say that the Council was defending the dignity of humanity against a radically pessimistic view of human nature. In other words the Council represents the view that human beings are expected to collaborate in their own salvation which is ultimately dependent on the work of Christ. The Lutheran view as suggested here is that human beings can do nothing for their own salvation, all is of God and Christ. You will find the same argument taking place in another religious tradition. Units 7–10 introduce you to the dispute in Hinduism between advocates of the 'cat principle' and those advocating the 'monkey principle', the former resembling the Lutheran and the generally Protestant position and the latter resembling the Catholic position.

5.2 The Christian religion after the Reformation

For the remainder of this part, I would like you to read certain sections of the *Encyclopedia* as I refer to them below. We do not have the opportunity to go into the detailed history of the Christian religion up to our time. The references in the following paragraphs should give you a sufficient basis to study Part Two, where we study in more detail certain aspects of the Christian religion, historically and contemporaneously. Make notes on key issues as you go along so that you can refer back to them easily.

By the end of the sixteenth century in Europe and within a short time in other parts of the world, most notably North America, the hegemony enjoyed by the Roman Catholic Church in the West was broken. Thereafter, while Rome remained powerful and major new energies were injected into her operations in Europe and abroad, especially through agencies like the Society of Jesus (see *Encyclopedia*, pp.133–6), and while she remained the largest single grouping within the Christian religion, with a huge programme of expansion worldwide (see *Encyclopedia*, pp.136–7), the Protestant elements in the Christian religion grew fairly rapidly and became powerful. One of the most significant developments in Protestantism after the direct emergence of those denominations from the Reformations was the emergence of the Methodist Church, the result of a pietistic movement which began in the Church of England, under the leadership of John and Charles Wesley. (See entries on the 'Wesleys' and 'Methodism' in the index of the *Encyclopedia.*)

The British Empire showed the political might of the Church of England, even if its numbers always remained fairly small in world terms. The USA slowly became powerful also and many Protestant denominations grew strong. Financially and politically, the American sphere of influence spread over the Pacific, while Africa became a major area of Christian expansion, often in competition with a resurgent Islam (see *Encyclopedia,* pp.120–3). In the USA, the pioneering and frontier mentality manifested itself in the Christian religion with innumerable Protestant-type denominations growing over the last two hundred years (see *Encyclopedia,* pp.114–5). Catholicism also grew in the USA through migration from Ireland and other European countries, most notably Italy and Poland, but its influence was slow to grow, although in numerical terms it could challenge the larger Protestant denominations. More recently the Roman Catholic Church in America has shown itself to be rather independent of the influence of Rome. This is especially evident in issues of individual morality and human rights, especially as they relate to the status of women generally and within the church. The Eastern Orthodox churches, mostly independent in their government and leadership, held on to their territories and only spread abroad to the new world in comparatively small numbers. In the recent past, many of the Orthodox churches have had to exist within their own territories under communist, officially atheistic regimes, and have played a role in the nationalist movements which have contributed to the break-up of the former Soviet Union (see *Encyclopedia,* pp.92–3; *Reader* 2.26). By this century we have a picture of an infinitely divided and dividing religion, while at the same time we have moves in the Protestant sphere of influence, occasionally successful, to unite into larger groupings (see *Encyclopedia,* pp.123–6, 161–2).

The Christian religion has had a struggle, sometimes very bitter, to come to terms with modernity. This struggle has been evident in the realm of the status of the scriptures as guides for living in modern times (see *Encyclopedia,* pp.115–20). It has been especially difficult to cope with the critical scrutiny of linguistic and theological scholars. Attacks on religion generally, and on the Christian religion in particular, have been commonplace since at least the eighteenth century and the experience has been unpleasant for the adherents of the religion. For many of the adherents, however, the seeming attack on the religion from within by scholars, including some who are responsible for pastoral leadership, has been even more painful. (For the Protestant side of the issue see *Encyclopedia,* pp.111–13, 126–7; and for the Roman Catholic side see *Encyclopedia,* pp.137–42, 145–6.)

It may also be argued that the economic basis of modernity – the expansion of capitalism – has disrupted traditional patterns of religious life. As the churches face the next millennium, many new challenges are being met with creative responses. Globalization, international migration and the post-colonial global political order have all led to a changed and heightened awareness of religious diversity, economic inequality, and of the complex relations between religion, culture, politics and economics. Inter-faith dialogue, the development of local forms of Christian spirituality and practice, intensified programmes of evangelization, black theology (*Reader* 2.24) and liberation theology (*Reader* 2.23) can each be seen as different responses to this changing awareness (see also *Encyclopedia,* pp.162–3).

In correlation with the emancipation of women, feminist theology has developed throughout the world to challenge all aspects of Christian faith and practice, from the doctrine of God, the nature of salvation, to the organization and leadership of Christian communities (*Reader* 2.20, 2.22). Here, as elsewhere, traditional sources are used and reinterpreted (*Reader* 2.21). The challenges of modern science have also met with a range of responses from Christians, from the fundamentalist rejection of Darwin and adherence to six-day creationism (belief that the creation took place in six days), through to the systematic treatises of theologians such as Wolfhart Pannenburg and Sallie McFague (see Further Reading list in the Update supplement). In particular, a narrative approach to theology, which stresses the function of stories in making sense of all of life from physics to romance, holds the promise of transcending the rift between facts and values which is part of the legacy of the Enlightenment, and hence of breaking down barriers between religion and science (see Stroup, 1981, and MacIntyre, 1981).

PART TWO: CHRISTIANITY AS A WORLD RELIGION

6 General considerations

In Part Two we will study the Christian religion from a number of perspectives and seek answers to these core questions.

(a) How does the religion exist in relation to authoritative, foundation figures and texts?

(b) How is the religion manifested according to some of the categories employed in the analysis of religion in the history of religions (for example, sacred space, sacred time, sacred persons)?

(c) How is the divine or the transcendent perceived by its adherents within the structure of the religion?

(d) Do the structure and organization of the religion reflect the ways in which belief and behaviour are perceived by the adherents?

As you read this part keep these questions constantly before you and make notes in the form of answers to these questions as they relate to the different topics studied.

Finally we will review the two units briefly by applying three key questions given in the Course Guide.

6.1 Institutions and organizations

In sections 2–4, you studied something of the life and teaching of Jesus Christ and of the life of the community that arose as a result of that life and teaching. At one stage the question of whether Jesus was the founder of the Christian religion was raised. The claim that he rose from the dead and had association with those who are referred to as his disciples is used as a sanction for the things that happened after his death. The major problem is that we only know of the things that are claimed to have happened after his death and which influenced further developments in the foundation of a movement, and then of a church or churches, through the testimony of those who were involved in these developments.

The setting up of the organization of the early church is in large part based on an event (the death and resurrection of Jesus) which is open to a variety of interpretations. There is also the problem of determining what was the intention of Jesus in proclaiming his message. Did he intend the setting up of an organization, in particular the setting up of a religion? It is not clear. The evidence is that he thought that there were those standing listening to him who would 'not taste death before they see the Kingdom of God come with power', a reference to the final days or the eschaton (the last event). Interpreting these words of Jesus has remained a problem of the Christian religion ever since.

There is a simple explanation which is offered by some scholars, namely that Jesus, in the heightened state of the prophetic experience, really did believe that the end was about to happen, but that he was mistaken. If this be the case then the argument against his having made provision for an organization is strengthened. A more traditional interpretation is that Jesus was referring to the receiving of the Holy Spirit at Pentecost, an interpretation which fits with Paul's understanding of the experience of the Spirit as the 'first fruits' of the eschaton. Although it may be argued that it was not the intention of Jesus to set up an organization let alone a religion, one cannot then go on to argue that the Christian religion is all a mistake.

We must take account of the message and the need felt by his followers to perpetuate that message. Given that motivation, not only is it not surprising that an organization emerged, but it is also not surprising that a religion emerged.

There is a similar situation in the life of Guru Nanak and the foundation of the Sikh religion (as you will discover in Units 14–15). There, too, we have a message, understood as divine revelation. The message and messenger have about them a charismatic quality. It becomes imperative for the followers, called disciples in both instances, to take steps to perpetuate the message through an institution. That a charismatic situation is at the heart of the matter is evidenced by the stories told about the teacher/prophet, stories that give a heightened view of his personality, his actions and the effect of his presence on the environment. In order to perpetuate the message and influence of the prophet, certain formulae are introduced. In Christianity these include 'Jesus is Lord', rituals based on events in his life, his baptism by John and his last meal with his followers, which became, in the case of baptism, the mode of entry into the new society, and in the case of the last meal, the institution of a sacred meal, the later eucharist, as a bonding mechanism for the new society. As the institution grows and develops it meets new situations which call for decisions. The decisions have to deal with situations unforeseen by the founder but have to be in tune with what they think would be the founder's intentions. So the new organization introduces ideas in the name of the founder and these get added to the corpus of material which comes from the founder himself. This may sound like cheating but it is not in so far as the leaders of the new organization believe that they are acting 'in the Spirit' of the founder. (In later doctrine this Spirit is identified as the third person of the Holy Trinity.) The sort of text that provides the legitimation for this procedure is found in the Fourth Gospel where Jesus is attributed the words:

> I have yet many things to say to you, but you cannot bear them now. When the Spirit of truth comes, he will guide you into all the truth; for he will not speak on his own authority, but whatever he hears he will speak, and he will declare to you things that are to come.
>
> (*John* 16:12–13)

An important fact to remember when considering the institutionalization of a movement such as the one that arose out of the message of Jesus Christ is that for ever after there is a constant tension between the demands of the message and the activities of the medium for the message, that is, the institution. When the tension becomes very acute it often results in attempts to recover what is thought to be the original message. Such attempts may be called reformations or revivals. These events affect not only the way the message is presented. The demand and commitment to the message may be heightened as in a revival, or the events may even affect the whole structure of the institution as in a reformation. The integration of message and medium is seen acutely in such an event.

6.2 Message, messenger and medium

Reference has been made to the message and the messenger. What is the message? Initially the message was about the kingdom of God and its coming. The messenger, Jesus Christ, spoke a great deal about it and we have stressed above one aspect of this eschatological message. The perpetuation of the message, however, involved very little reference to the kingdom of God and much more to the death and resurrection of Jesus Christ. (See again section 2.) The messenger is now a different person. He is the apostle Paul, or the authors of other documents in the New Testament.

The message has taken on a plurality of emphases with much written about the way of salvation, the life of the church, the behaviour required of the believers, and various interpretations of the person and work of Jesus Christ. Apart from the gospels, the so-called 'good news' documents, the rest of the message or messages are carried in the form of letters, actual letters or letter-style documents, some of them more like minor treatises, and a rather strange document entitled 'The Apocalypse of John (the Divine)'. This collection of documents was soon accorded the status of sacred writing. The scriptures are part of the institutionalizing process. Teaching, advice, commentary, mostly of an *ad hoc* nature originally, are given permanent shape and an abiding authority. One of the qualities of sacred writing is its authoritativeness. In the case of the Christian religion, and as you will see in the Sikh religion, not only are the words of the charismatic teacher/prophet collected, formalized and given authoritative power, but so too the words of the first followers and leaders of the organization. Power is given to documents bearing the names of such persons.

The New Testament, which included the teacher/prophet Jesus' own words, and the other documents which are in a sense an extended commentary on his words, and the Old Testament, the Hebrew scriptures which contain the record of God's activities in preparing the way for God's central act, the calling of Jesus of Nazareth to be Son and Saviour of the world, are the foundation documents for all activities, both individual and corporate, thereafter. It should be noted that the sacred writings which are the foundation documents of subsequent developments down to this day are themselves the products of the early developments. This is an interesting point for the student of religion, and raises issues concerning the foundation of a religion. This is the case in all religions where sacred writings are the foundation of religious belief and religious institutions.

6.3 Sacred writings

The *canon* of scripture, from the Greek meaning 'measured rod,' is the corpus of documents accepted as authoritative by the one church initially, subsequently by the churches of the East and West, and eventually by churches on each side of the Protestant divide, except for those books accepted as authoritative by Rome and the Eastern churches but rejected by the Protestant churches, including the Church of England, which are not in the Hebrew Bible and go under the title 'The Apocrypha'. Apart from the Apocrypha the Bible is accepted as uniquely authoritative by almost the whole of the Christian religion.

In considering the development of the religion institutionally and organizationally we should remember the authoritative role of the scriptures. The majority of Christians would regard the Bible as in some sense 'the Word of God'. Within that general categorization attitudes and beliefs will vary considerably. At one extreme we find that the phrase is applied literally, in the sense that it is believed that God literally spoke every word in the Bible, Old and New Testaments, as dictation to the prophet, to the apostle, through Jesus Christ and whatever other medium was employed. This literalism extends not only to the original languages, but also to the translations and down to the punctuation marks. At the other extreme we find that the phrase means that the Bible generally manifests the mind and will of God, but that to press the literalist standpoint ignores the real problems of variant manuscripts, and the problem of deciding what the correct text is in a particular instance, and adopts a view of God's dealing with people which resembles more a puppet-master and puppet relationship rather than a creator and a creature of free-will. The extremes reflect attitudes which range from an almost magical application of the text of the Bible to the general acceptance of the truths of scripture in so far as they accord with human reason.

In churches with a liturgical tradition the scriptures play an integral part in worship with an uncritical application of them going back to a pre-critical period. In churches or organizations which do not have a basis of liturgy based on pre-Reformation practice the same authority of scripture is observed. The language of prayer in liturgical and non-liturgical settings tends to be heavily dependent on biblical language. The structure of worship in both settings reflects the theology of the tradition and its beliefs as to what a church is and how it should respond to what it considers divine initiative.

6.4 The unity of the church

In sections 2–4 we studied the rise of the early organization which was called 'the church'. We have seen in section 5 how some scholars regard the importance of the unity of the church and the anomalies in some views of what constitutes that unity. The earliest accounts we have of the organization which arose in the wake of the experience of the resurrection of Jesus Christ from the dead seem to suggest that though there was in a sense a unity of experience, there was not a unity of organization. The early travels of someone like Paul meant that churches were set up as a result of his appeal to local populations to follow the teaching and to experience the life of Jesus. There was no single organization. Local congregations threw up local leaders who were usually called presbyters, or elders, and there was in some places a notion of *episkope*, oversight, from which comes the English term 'bishop'. As was pointed out in section 4.3 the term *episkopos* is used coterminously with presbyter in the New Testament, and both refer to the leadership, or superintendence of the local church in that context. As feminist scholars have pointed out, it is significant that some of the *presbyteroi* and *diakanoi* (another term for minister), and even one apostle (Junia, *Romans* 16:7), mentioned by Paul in his letters are female, a fact that is often obscured by translating these terms in relation to a woman as 'helper', suggesting a subordinate role. In the cast of Junia, later editions and translations even change the gender of the name to Junias, a male form of the name unparalleled in contemporary literature, to avoid the conclusion that Paul could possibly refer to an apostle as a woman. (Those interested in exploring this point are referred to Fiorenza, 1983, especially pp.168–75.)

Later, presbyter seems to give way to bishop and we find the development of an office which controls church organization. In particular, the bishop has the sole responsibility for the celebration of the eucharist. Within a short time priests are able to celebrate the rite but only with the authority of the bishop. This marks the early stage of the unity of church organization under the authority of bishops. In order to counteract heresies Ecumenical Councils were held, the first being that of Nicaea in 325. Though the Bishop of Rome gained pre-eminence, he was never completely accepted by the church in the Eastern Roman Empire. Thereafter 'the church' means 'the One Holy and Apostolic Church', but not for very long. Though Christians belonging to certain traditions have never ceased to recite creeds which proclaim the unity of the church, this has been more in hope than achievement.

6.5 The church: the One Body

The term 'church' has its roots in two Greek words. The first is the term *kyriakon* (belonging to the Lord), and the second is *ekklesia* (gathering or being called together). The latter word has some of the connotations of the term synagogue. If we take the two Greek words together then we have an institution which has the Lord (Jesus Christ) as a reference point and is by nature a group of people drawn together, out of the larger grouping to which people belong through normal association in society.

Although there is no uniform pattern to the church in the New Testament the metaphor that attached itself to the church then, namely that it is the body of Christ (*Ephesians* 1:22–3), has been the theological basis of belief in the church ever since. In section 4.3.1 reference was made to *1 Corinthians* 12 and the different forms of ministry referred to in that chapter. The context of the list of ministries is the metaphor of the church as the body of Christ.

> For just as the body is one and has many members, and all the members of the body, though many, are one body, so it is with Christ. For by one Spirit we were all baptized into one body – Jews and Greeks, slaves or free – and all are made to drink of one spirit.
>
> (*1 Corinthians* 12:12–13)

The metaphor appears to stand for two things. First there is the social/spiritual aspect of the church wherein all differences of nationality and class are broken down (including the difference of gender). Secondly, there is the belief that by being baptized into the body (that is the body of Christ), the believer enters into the salvation brought about by Christ through the sacrifice of his body on the Cross. The psychology of this metaphor is both Hebraic and Hellenistic. The Hebrew cannot conceive of the elimination of the body we inhabit in life. On the other hand the Hellenistic has a more mystical, less corporeal perception of the body and its relation to the hidden world. So in this metaphor we are reminded of Christ's broken body on the Cross and the body that ascended into heaven and sits at the right hand of God. The church by this metaphor is the body of Christ in the world, displaying his wounds, manifesting the power of his resurrection, perpetuating his teaching and the spirit of his teaching through example and mission, and being the 'first-fruits' of salvation. That is the theological picture, the ideal picture if you like, but still the picture which those who believe in 'the Church' try to work out in their social environment.

There is bound to be a tension within a body that believes it is on its way from this world to heaven. Some of the marks of heaven should be already present. The position of the church is very much one of 'it has happened but not fully'. The church is said to be held between the 'Now' and the 'Not yet'. The church is seen very much as a staging post from 'earth' to 'heaven'. Nowhere is this more evident than in the Orthodox Church, where the very architecture of the space where ritual is performed is a metaphor of the tension between the 'Now' and the 'Not yet'. (Look at Figure 1(a) on page 61; see also the programme 'Easter worship: the Greek liturgy' on video cassette 1.) The lines dividing the space show especially the area which we may designate 'heaven'. It is the space that lies beyond the iconostasis, that is the screen on which are hung holy icons (paintings). We will look in more detail at other models of sacred space in section 8.1.

6.6 The 'Church' and the churches

We have already noted that although the creeds acknowledged by the major Christian traditions talk of the 'One, Holy, Catholic and Apostolic Church', based on the notion of the One Body of Christ, in history we have a multiplicity of churches. In the first instance we have the major divisions between Rome and Orthodoxy, with the latter divided into a number of autocephalous churches, that is, churches with their own titular head (see *Encyclopedia*, p.90). Then, in the West and in areas influenced by western churches, we have divisions too numerous to count, and still dividing, though in some cases uniting. This global pattern of division must raise questions of what relation, if any, there is between 'the Church as the Body of Christ' and all these churches. A common response in traditions other than the Roman and extreme Evangelicalism is that these divisions are scandalous and everything should be done to bring about organic unity. The Roman view also sees the scandal of divisions and in the Second Vatican Council (1962) recognizes that there are 'separated brethren' who share a 'sacramental bond' through baptism (see section 8.5), but lack the 'fullness of unity' because their ministers are not properly ordained and therefore cannot unite in the eucharist. (For an account of the Second Vatican Council, see *Encyclopedia*, pp.154ff.) Nevertheless the Decree on Ecumenism presses for unity to be sought, a unity in which zeal does not displace truth. Many Evangelical Protestants have tended to ignore moves towards Christian unity, when they are not attacking those seeking unity, often on the grounds that the churches concerned, not being firm adherents to the truth of the Gospel as they understand it, are not true churches. For such Christians being separated is a virtue. There are also, however, organizations, such as the Evangelical Alliance, that seek to draw together Evangelical Protestant Christians from various churches.

The clearest expression of the response that divisions are scandalous and that something should be done to restore unity is found generally in the twentieth-century ecumenical movement and in particular since 1948 in the World Council of Churches. (See again *Encyclopedia*, pp.161–3.) The World Council has experienced great difficulties in advancing the unity of the different traditions, though it has been active in promoting response to world social and political issues. In this respect it has become a voice to speak for the non-Roman Christian world. However, in spite of its early promise of solving the ambiguities of a divided Christian religion, the Council has failed to come up with the necessary power to back up the theology it has expressed over the years.

In those traditions that are associated with the Council there have been some notable unions, the most significant being the churches of South India, North India and Pakistan. These were unions of certain Protestant churches with the local area of the Anglican church. In each case there were important churches which did not join the union. In South India a significant Lutheran church did not unite and in North India neither did a significant Methodist church of American extraction. In Britain, Canada and the USA there have been important though less significant unions between Presbyterians and Congregationalists. In Britain there was a union of three Methodist churches in 1932, but the attempt to unite the Church of England and the present Methodist Church failed badly and a similar move in Wales (but of wider scope) also failed. The failures have tended to become institutionalized. The path to unity thus seems difficult and slow.

The unions in North and South India took place after years (in the case of North India after decades) of negotiation over the constitution of the proposed church, episcopal ordination and doctrinal details of the eucharist. During the sixties a mood began to grow which suggested that adherents to the Christian religion in many parts were impatient at the prospect of protracted negotiation and more interested in spiritual rather than constitutional union. In its most developed form this mood gave rise to the 'charismatic movement' in many of the mainline churches. (See *Encyclopedia*, pp.164–5.) These churches are now faced with thousands of members whose main driving force is the awareness of fellowship with like-minded Christians, an enthusiasm expressed in singing songs with popular rhythms, speaking with tongues (that is, speaking an incomprehensible language under the influence of the Holy Spirit) (cf. the experience of the apostles on the first Pentecost after the Resurrection, *Acts* 2:1–4), and whose doctrine consists mainly of a pietistic account of a belief that Jesus is alive in their midst. This movement crosses all denominational boundaries, even the Catholic/Protestant divide.

Worldwide there is a great deal of collaboration between churches. In many places the prospective ministers of the various churches study and train together. Issues such as opposition to apartheid in South Africa have brought adherents of different churches together even to the point of sharing prison together (see *Reader* 2.24, 2.25). In the face of so much belligerence in the world between major and minor powers, the leaders and the laity recognize the need for expressions of solidarity of opinion and commitment to try to combat racism, poverty and conflict. There is a great deal of common activity which many consider now to be more important and more effective as an opportunity for a richer plurality, which is more realistic in the contemporary world, and which may be seen as more creative and responsive to the world's needs.

6.7 Church order

In section 6.1 it was pointed out that there often arises a tension between the message of Christ and the institution which carries that message. When the tension becomes acute, then reformations and revivals can occur. In the case of reformations the attempt to recover the original message can lead to structural changes in the institution, resulting in a reformed institution (as in the case with the Roman Church after the Council of Trent) or in a plurality of institutions set up by those who thought that they could not hope for a sufficient measure of reform in respect of the message, even in a reformed church. The picture of church order – the way churches are governed – that emerges from the Protestant Reformation is as various as the institutions themselves. In some instances claims are made that a return to primitive New Testament order has been achieved. In many cases no such claim is made and order is based on the pattern of secular order that prevails in the institution's territory.

In the Roman Church very little structural change actually occurred, most of the reform being directed at the way the message was to be presented in word and ritual. The primacy and the infallibility of the Pope speaking *ex cathedra* remained (see *Reader* 2.16). In more recent times the importance of collegiality has been stressed. Collegiality stresses the importance of the bishops, who have always had considerable authority in their own dioceses under the Pope, sharing to a limited extent in consultation with the Pope in the way the church should behave universally in the contemporary world. There are signs that bishops in certain countries (the Netherlands, Britain and the USA) wish to see a development from mere consultation to a greater degree of authority and government as in the Orthodox churches (see the *Encyclopedia*, pp.85–6 and 90–2).

The removal of a priestly hierarchy in Protestantism has produced various democratic forms of church order. Lutheran churches are very often closely bound to the state, the head of state being the chief authority in the church. There is only one order of clergy, in some countries examined and provided for by the government. The chief officials in the German Lutheran churches are titled 'General Superintendents', though the title bishop is also used, as it is in Denmark and Sweden. The government of the churches is in the hands of synods consisting of clerical and lay members. In state churches religious questions are settled either by secular legislation or consistory courts.

Presbyterianism has a very detailed government structure. At the lowest level is the local church and its government shared by the minister and the elders. In Scotland this is the Kirk Session. Above this lies the Presbytery, the body responsible for the areas covered by a number of local congregations. Then comes the Synod which covers a number of Presbyteries, and finally the General Assembly which is the legislative body of the whole church. The responsibilities of the courts below the General Assembly consist in implementing the policies agreed at the General Assembly, maintaining and propagating the faith in line with the Assembly interpretations and administering discipline in the name of the Assembly. It is the Assembly that is responsible for the acceptance and ordination of ministers. At each level of government there is an appropriate mix of clerical and lay representation. In Scotland 'the Church' is the state church established by law.

The structure of the Methodist Church is based on the arrangements made by John Wesley for those groups which had grown up in his lifetime. There are those who claim that its form of government is essentially presbyterian. The supreme body of the Methodist Church in Britain, constituted under state law, is the Conference. It is made up of an equal number of ministers and laity. In matters dealing with the ministers there is a separate 'Ministerial Session'. Decisions affecting the whole church are taken in full Conference, the 'Representative Session'. The President of the Conference, always a minister, and the Vice-President, always a lay person, are elected annually by Conference. The church is divided into districts which have their own synods. Each district is made up of a number of circuits, which in turn are made up of a number of 'societies'. Methodism is found in many areas of the world, but the most significant from the point of view of order is the church in the USA with its offshoots in countries such as India. John Wesley 'set apart' Thomas Coke to superintend the Methodist societies in the USA. Coke ordained another member to share the superintendence, but also adopted the title 'bishop' against Wesley's wishes. As a consequence the Methodist Church in the USA (with its offshoots) is uniquely episcopal.

The more radical Protestant denominations and sects generally observe a localized form of government. Baptist churches, for example, are governed by the local congregation through elected deacons governing with the minister. Larger regional or national bodies, such as the Baptist Union, exist more as an expression of solidarity in a common purpose than legislative bodies with power or authority over the local congregation. Some activities, such as the training of ministers, and increasingly the creation of central funds for the financial maintenance of the ministry, bind such congregations together. It is the local church which calls and commissions the ministers, though there will be other ministers of the denomination who will join in the ordination.

Nearly all these Protestant churches have relations with their fellow denominationalists throughout the world. These world organizations serve the function of being a forum for common decisions and mutual support.

Even more radical Christian groupings can be found which are completely and singularly autonomous owing no allegiance nor even acknowledging a fellowship with any body or bodies outside their own congregation. Some of these congregations are the creation of the minister or charismatic leader. In these cases it is probably more appropriate to call them sects rather than churches, though they themselves would often call themselves churches on the grounds that they replicate the gathered 'ecclesia' of the New Testament, owing no allegiance to any bishop or court but simply to Jesus Christ.

Finally we look at the organization of the churches within the Anglican Communion. The Church of England is unique in being the only church within the Communion which is a state church, established by law. As such it has the monarch as temporal head and important changes within the church, such as liturgical reform, are subject to the approval of Parliament. Of course, the church is usually allowed to have its say in its own affairs, and much of the legislation and policy of the Church of England is determined initially by its synods, formerly one of Canterbury and one of York, now the General Synod. In other parts of the Communion the churches have either been disestablished, as in Ireland and Wales, or have always had an existence separate from the Crown. In these parts of the Communion a more clearly democratic organization prevails. Each church within the Anglican Communion, while recognizing a traditional primacy residing in Canterbury, is completely autonomous. Every ten years a Conference is convened in Lambeth in London of all the bishops of the Anglican Communion, the chairman, as a matter of tradition, being the Archbishop of Canterbury. The Lambeth Conference has no juridical authority over the member churches, though to some extent it has moral authority.

In its encounter with 'the world' nowhere does the Christian religion appear to be more worldly than in its institutional organization. The extreme form of 'worldliness' for some people, probably for many Christians including Roman Catholics, is the fact that the Vatican, the headquarters of the Roman Catholic Church worldwide, is a city and a state, like any other secular state, with its ambassadors or nuncios with diplomatic status in the capitals of the world.

Yet it is difficult to see, the Vatican apart, how the Christian religion could survive and prosper without the institutional structure that we find today. It is true that these institutional structures are a constant source of discomfort to adherents of the religion, especially if the income of a church depends on investments which derive profits from morally questionable sources such as breweries. Given the complexities of modern multinational business concerns it is extremely difficult for the churches to be seen to have clean hands. The ambiguities of being 'the Church in the World' are constantly present in the Christian religion. Quite how it, or any other religion for that matter, could exist without these ambiguities is difficult to see.

7 Religious leadership

7.1 Sacred persons

Every religion manifests some aspect of the general category of sacred person. In 4.3 'Church order and ministry', and 4.4 'Ascetics and monks', you were introduced to forms of sacred persons as they appeared in the earliest centuries of the Christian religion. In examining this topic further we will need to reiterate some of what was said in 4.3 and to elaborate a little further on the religious thinking found in the New Testament

It is true that up until the Protestant Reformation the western church had a basic structure of bishop, priest and deacon. In Latin, the official language of the Roman Church still, the word for priest is *sacerdos* which brings out the holiness and by implication the sacrificial nature of the office in a way that the English word priest (presbyter) does not, though it is understood that the English word priest has always been used for those religious contexts where sacrifice is performed. In the Greek Orthodox Church the title is *hiereus*, which also has sacrificial connotations. In the Church of England, though the sacrificial connotation was not revived until the nineteenth century under the influence of the Oxford Movement (see *Encyclopedia*, pp.112–3), the official title of the most common office always remained that of priest. In Welsh the title even after the Reformation has always been *offeiriad*, in which English speakers may recognize the root of the word 'offer', that is, offer a sacrifice. In this respect again, the Church of England and its derivatives have been different from the other Protestant churches. It is true that in the service of ordination to the priesthood there has never been a suggestion that the office involves any sacrifice and the person ordained is ordained to the *ministry* of the church. In typical Anglican style the office is that of a priest, the work that of a minister.

Other titles in common use are pastor or preacher. The former title accentuates the caring nature of the office with its reminder that pastor is the Latin for shepherd, a title given to Jesus. The term is used in some radical Protestant churches as a formal title. The term preacher is a more vernacular title, but again used mainly in more radical Protestant traditions. There are Christian organizations which use none of these titles. The Society of Friends does not have a formalized ministry and has no one who could carry a title. The Salvation Army, as its name might suggest, has formal leaders who take military ranks.

These titles on the whole reflect the perceived significance of the work done by the holder of the title. Where the title 'priest' is used there will be a tendency to view the work as in some sense participating in an act related to the death of Christ viewed as a sacrifice. Where the title 'minister' is used there will generally be emphasis more on the serving nature of the office, ministering to the spiritual needs of the community. The same applies to the title pastor. Preacher obviously shows the dominance of the office holder as a purveyor of words, homiletics, the interpretation of scripture.

7.2 The priesthood

7.2.1 Let us look in more detail at the oldest and, in some senses, the most universal perception of sacred persons in the Christian religion, which I will gather up under the category of priesthood. This category covers not only the office of priests but also bishops. I will not deal with deacons who lie outside the priesthood and are restricted in the rituals they are allowed to perform. I will not deal either with ascetics, monks and nuns, though there have been developments over the centuries since the period covered in 4.4. First, please refer back to 4.3 and re-read what was said there.

7.2.2 One may look at the priesthood of the Christian churches under two aspects, which combine in the office of priest as it relates to the person and work of Jesus Christ. First there is the fact that in some sense the Christian priest is the successor to the priest of the older Hebrew religion. In Judaism before 70 CEwhen the last temple in Jerusalem was destroyed, there was a priesthood; there were priests officiating in the Jerusalem temple in the time of Jesus. There were also rabbis performing a different function within Judaism, and when the temple was destroyed and sacrifice ceased, the rabbis were already in a position to take over leadership in the Jewish religion (see Units 1–2 section 2). Jesus himself, according to the Fourth Gospel, appears to some of his contemporaries in the tradition of the rabbis. Certainly much of his teaching echoes that of rabbis who predated him. The New Testament office of presbyter relates directly to the synagogue life of Judaism and the rabbinical tradition.

In the early church, however, Jesus was thought of as the great high priest of God. Strictly speaking there is no priesthood in the Christian religion in the technical, Hebrew sense, but in the new dispensation in which the old is superseded in the life and death of Jesus Christ it is held that there is a priesthood which far exceeds the old in its efficacy. The references to this superior priesthood are found in the *Epistle to the Hebrews.*

> The former priests were many in number, because they were prevented by death from continuing in office; but he [the Christ] holds his priesthood permanently, because he continues for ever ... For it was fitting that we should have such a high priest, holy, blameless, unstained, separated from sinners, exalted high above the heavens. He has no need, like those high priests, to offer sacrifices daily, first for his own sins and then for those of the people; he did this once when he offered up himself.
>
> (*Hebrews* 7:23–27; see also *Reader* 2.5.2)

According to this interpretation Jesus Christ is both high priest and sacrifice of the new dispensation. The result of this interpretation of the status of Christ is that all those who believe in the saving power of his sacrifice become themselves a priesthood, a priesthood of all believers (*1 Peter* 2:5; *Revelation* 1:6). The Greek *hiereus* and its cognates, which stands for the priest in the old Hebrew sense, is used only twice in the New Testament, once for Christ himself and once for those who believe through him. There is no suggestion that the term can apply to any holder of office within the rudimentary organization which follows the resurrection of Christ. This fact will be seen as important as we follow through our discussion. We now pick up the discussion of points introduced in section 4.3.

7.2.3 The church in the third and fourth centuries underwent a change in self-image from synagogue to temple, and with it came a transformation in the understanding of the role of presbyter. The bishop, it should be realized, is basically a presbyter with responsibilities of oversight. In the beginning there was no additional *order* of bishops. First there were bishops who were set apart, then, as presbyters multiplied, there was a setting apart of a priest for the office of bishop. In the transformation priests and bishops were no longer seen as deriving their priesthood from the body of the faithful, from the holy priesthood which derives its priesthood from Christ. The priesthood of Christ was now understood to be conferred directly through ordination. There may have been many reasons for this. It is likely that the clergy themselves would have been led to enhance their own status and holiness. On the other hand, since much of Christian doctrine and the action of the hierarchy have arisen from the attitudes and devotions of the adherents, one reason might have been popular pressure for the religious leaders to be seen as more separated, more holy, more clearly to be persons with holy gifts and able to offer more reliable sacramental, even quasi-magical, services to the faithful. There is a pressure and a tendency in all religions for the symbols of transcendence to be concretized, to be invested with the power they symbolize, actually to be powerful to the touch or by presence. An object that is held to possess such power is called a talisman. The attitude towards the divine and the availability of the divine manifested in the use of a talisman is present in many different ways and applies not only to such objects as charms or amulets but also to persons, places and events. It is this tendency, which will be referred to in these units as the talismanic tendency, that lies behind much of the development in the early to medieval Christian churches.

7.2.4 One must also remember that over these centuries the Christian religion was expanding. Tribes were being converted but these new Christians would often not be completely converted. They would have preserved their sacred places and sacred devotions, in new Christian clothing no doubt, but the body underneath would still have been significantly pre-Christian. To think that the Christian religion completely eliminated these inherited sanctities is to misunderstand the process of religious expansion. We are only gradually learning what popular religion was like in these centuries. In the Middle Ages 'Popular belief attached itself to the concrete and the seen, not because the faith of the people was materialistic, but because for them matter was an expression of spiritual forces. Holiness was real because one could see its effects' (Aston, 1981, p.159). This situation did not just emerge in the Middle Ages. It was present some centuries earlier and such pressure would have affected the response of the clergy. The tradition of celibate priesthood in the Latin West (what was to become the Roman Catholic Church after 1054) also deserves mention here. The admiration of sexual continence was universal to the church from the early centuries, but this was primarily exercised in terms of post-marital celibacy. But from the late sixth century in the West wives disappear from the households of clergy, and most bishops come from the monasteries. Those interested in exploring further the impact of Christianity on perceptions of sexuality should read Brown (1988).

7.2.5 In the Middle Ages the role of the priest became increasingly holy. The actions performed by the priest took on new depths of holiness, of efficacy in holiness. The things he touched were holy. The ritual space he occupied became holy. In the true sense of holiness he, and the things he touched ritually, became more and more separated from the laity as the priest's holiness increased. The sense of ritual purity was heightened in relation to the priest's office. This purity bore no relation to his actual moral attitude or behaviour. His ordination as priest, that is, his setting apart from profane life, guaranteed the efficacy of his actions. The ritual space became more holy through a combination of its occupation by a sacred person and its occupation by the divine presence, the Host (from the Latin *hostia* meaning sacrificial victim, the bread or wafer which becomes sacred after consecration). It was installed and hidden from sight in an earlier phase and up until today in a tabernacle, a small decorated cupboard-like receptacle, on the altar. Increasingly in the later Middle Ages and up until today, it is displayed visibly in a monstrance, a receptacle with a glass-sided section, again on the altar, where it can be seen and be the object of adoration by the faithful as the 'real presence' of the 'real' Body and blood of Jesus

Christ. It is also the visible evidence of the sacerdotalism which entered the Christian religion during the Dark and Middle Ages and which reached its pinnacle shortly before the onset of the Protestant Reformation.

7.2.6 In order to produce the 'real' Body of Christ the action which brought about the 'Body' of Christ had to be re-enacted. The original action was the death of Christ on the Cross seen as a sacrifice for the sins of the human race. The resulting mystical 'Body' was from the beginning a powerful symbol of salvation and the route of salvation was to be initiated through baptism. As Paul said, 'to be baptized into his death', to participate in the eucharist, 'to receive the Body and Blood of Christ', thereby to be incorporated into his Body. This spiritual journey, relying on the efficacy of symbols in a truly sacramental way, proved inadequate, as we have seen. The devout needed the 'real' thing and in order to receive the real thing not only was there pressure for the concretization of the object of salvation, but the action which brought about the concrete object also had to be reproduced somehow. So the priest became collaborator in the sacrifice, a sacrifice re-enacted in each celebration of the Mass. Though the Catholic Reformation removed many of the abuses which provoked the Protestant Reformation the sacerdotalism of the priesthood remained and still remains.

7.2.7 So far we have concentrated on the priesthood in the western (Roman) church. The situation in the Eastern Orthodox churches is similar in some respects but not in others. The development of sacrificial connotations in the earlier centuries was common to both East and West. The main difference is perhaps to be seen in the focal point of the community. The Orthodox position is briefly described by Zernov in *Encyclopedia*, pages 90 to 91. There he says that: 'Clergy and lay people are co-celebrants in the administration of the divine Mysteries, the purpose of which is to assist them in the process of their spiritual growth and to increase the power of love among them.' This, no doubt, is the doctrinal basis of the relationship between clergy and laity. It is true that there are lay as well as clerical theologians in Orthodoxy. However, the actual progression of church life at the parochial level is very much in the hands of the priest with the title of *hiereus* with its sacrificial connotations. The programme on the Easter liturgy on video cassette 1 demonstrates very clearly the relationship. While Zernov rightly emphasizes the important role played by the laity in the life of the church, in terms of its theology, teaching and government, in essence there is very little difference in the status enjoyed by the Orthodox priest relative to the Roman priest, and like the Roman priest that status has remained unchanged since the early centuries. In the Orthodox traditions clergy may be married but higher office is usually restricted to celibates. In both traditions the rite of ordination is held to confer on the ordained a special gift of the Spirit, whereby either the grace conferred in baptism is deepened or an extra power is conferred for the efficacious administration of the sacraments of the church. The role is essentially representative, in that Christ is represented in their office, and paternal in respect of the relationship with the laity, hence the use of the form of address 'Father' in both traditions.

7.3 Post-Reformation ministries

We have seen the close link between the religious status of the priest and the status of the rituals performed by the priest in the medieval church. The Protestant reformers attacked both aspects with varying results. In section 6 we looked at the question of authority and in section 8 we will look at the status of rituals. Here we will concentrate on those men, and later women, who come under the category of sacred person in the West after the

Reformation in the traditions other than the Roman. It may be part of our study to see if the category of sacred person is in fact meaningful in the context of the Protestant traditions. I will divide our study into three parts: moderate Protestant, radical Protestant, and catholic Protestant.

7.3.1 There is more than one way of describing the difference between the Roman and the various Protestant views of the sacred person. There is the major element of the protest made in Europe against the whole sacerdotal structure of the medieval church. There was an all-out attack on what has been called here the talismanic tendency. This tendency was attacked in simple evangelical terms as being contrary to all that Christ stood for in the way of bringing people to God. This work of Christ was seen as liberating human beings rather than holding them in thrall to what was seen as the quasi-magical powers invested in the priests through the power of the church. Not only was this thralldom seen in spiritual but also in material terms in that liberation was to be bought for a price. Grace had a price tag. Finally, a corollary of the desacralizing of the universe, of opening it up to science, was the desacralizing of human beings. The Protestant Reformation had a great deal to do with rejecting the possibility of any metaphysical change taking place, not only in such things as bread and wine, but also in people. The work of those who were to occupy the place of the sacred persons in the new traditions would be seen as purely functional, with no metaphysical change in the person, no notion of 'the indelible conferring of priesthood'. There was to be a notion of persons being 'set apart', but that phrase was not to bear the Old Testament meaning of intrinsic holiness; rather it was now to mean 'being available' to serve the community or the congregation.

'Catholics' have sometimes accused Protestants of so stressing 'the priesthood of all believers' that the priesthood is dragged down to the level of the laity so that there is no priesthood left. The Protestant response is to claim that on the contrary the laity were raised to the level of the priesthood. We can take one aspect of priesthood which became a central issue. It is what is customarily known as 'the power of the keys'. The reference is to the words addressed to Simon by Jesus (*Matthew* 16:13–20) that because Simon had recognized Jesus as the Christ he would be known henceforth as Peter, and to him would be given the keys of the kingdom of heaven which gave him power to loose or bind, that is, to forgive sins or not. To this day in the 'catholic' traditions (and here we include the Orthodox and Anglican), only a priest can pronounce forgiveness of sins. As far as Luther was concerned every Christian had the power of the keys, *but* should not exercise this authority unless publicly authorized to do so. This was broadly Calvin's view also.

The position with regard to preaching the Word of God was similar. The teaching of the Bible was clear and open to all, hence the importance of the Bible in the vernacular. For Luther the Christian preacher was a man 'set apart', 'an Angel of God' (*anggelos* in Greek means 'messenger'), 'a very bishop', 'a saviour', 'a king and prince in the kingdom of God'. 'There is nothing more precious or noble on earth and in this life than a true, faithful person or preacher.' For Calvin, God 'chooses from among men those who are his ambassadors to the world, to be the interpreters of his secret will, and even to act as his personal representatives'.

From this evidence it is wrong to depict either Luther or Calvin as having a 'weak' doctrine of the ministry of the church. The main differences are that the minister does not have sacerdotal powers. He acts by virtue of his calling by the whole church and acts as the representative of the church, not of the bishop. For both Calvin and Luther the position of the church under God was paramount and the ministry could only be carried out if it was regularized by and responsible to the church. At least that was the ideal principle. In fact, of course, while sacerdotalism was effectively kept out, the ministry, in spite of Protestant claims to the contrary, did become 'clericalized' fairly soon.

The word 'clerical' refers strictly to orders within episcopal traditions, but the term is often used to denote a particular professional approach or attitude of superiority to the laity in both episcopal and non-episcopal traditions. While clericalism was an obvious feature of the pre-Reformation church and continued in the 'catholic' traditions, it is also very difficult to avoid clericalism in Protestantism; even in the radical Protestant traditions. Luther and Calvin theologically asserted the primacy of the church under God, and in Calvin's case organizationally asserted the primacy of the presbyters. Nevertheless, having a high view of the minister, especially as preacher of the Word of God, is almost bound to lead to an attitude on the part of the laity that the minister is set apart in more than a functional sense. In the Lutheran tradition the title of parson, in German *Pfarrer*, and the parochial organization from which the title derives, meant that much of the respect and reverence for the erstwhile priest was carried over. Indeed the laity actually continued to employ the title of priest unofficially.

In both major moderate Protestant traditions, even as they have been broken down into smaller units of a localized (or as in the case of Scotland, national) organization the minister has enjoyed enhanced status. One way in which the status has been enhanced is in the standard of moral observance demanded of the minister. It is true that any form of immorality is a scandal in these traditions, but the offence experienced when a minister transgresses shows up the relative ineffectiveness of the doctrine of the priesthood of all believers. The whole priesthood is equal but the priesthood of some is more equal than others. Clericalism takes the place of sacerdotalism so that in a derived sense, if not in the technical sense, the category of the sacred person does carry over into the major moderate Protestant traditions. In Lutheranism in Germany and Sweden the retention of bishops and pastors served as a continuation of the sacredness of office. In Calvinism, although the fourfold order of preacher, teacher, elder and deacon has not carried over into all the Presbyterian churches, the normal pattern of minister and elder, with normally a presiding Moderator, has meant that a similar ethos of clericalism prevails.

In Lutheranism the clericalism is manifested in the retention or adaptation of the vesture of the pre-Reformation church. In Calvinism we find the more sober, even sombre, black gown of the preacher with white bands hanging at the neck. Though the ministers concerned may not normally wear an identifying vesture when not participating in divine worship, the adoption of the Roman collar (vulgarly known as a dog collar) has become quite widespread in Protestant traditions in this century. This marking out, this setting apart through dress if not by ordination, is something in which ministers often collude with the laity who demand that their ministers are not only deemed to be 'different', but seen to be different. Much of what has been said in this section could also be applied to the ministry of the Methodist church.

7.3.2 In many ways what has been said about the moderate Protestant ministry can also be applied to the radical type. The main visible difference in many cases would be the total absence of any form of ritual dress, not even a black preaching gown. It is as difficult to point to distinctive differences of doctrine concerning the radical ministries. About the only real difference is the even firmer rejection of sacerdotalism and of clericalism, the latter more theoretical than actual. There is, if anything, also a more diffuse sense of setting apart for the ministry. Whereas in the Lutheran and

Presbyterian traditions the 'call' to be a minister is to the whole church, in the radical traditions the call is to the local congregation. This has raised debate in ecumenical circles as to whether the minister's 'ordination' in such circumstances is a single, repeatable action, requiring a new 'ordination' each time a minister is called to a new charge. Under the influence of the ecumenical movement there has been a move in some churches towards a more formal acknowledgement of ordination as an action with ongoing effect, and the call to the local congregation takes on the nature of a change to take up new duties. One aspect of the whole issue is that as membership of churches has tended to decline and the financial support of the minister has become a problem (resulting in more centralized arrangements and the grouping of pastorates), then a more formalized view of the ministry has taken place. The central body which pays at least part of the minister's salary tends to take a more active role in the charging of the minister and of his move from one pastorate to another. Resistance to sacerdotalism has been more successful than the resistance to clericalism, and what was said of the Lutheran and Presbyterian traditions in this respect can be repeated here, even to the increasing adoption of ritual dress by ministers in the radical traditions.

An interesting development of 'clericalism' is seen in television evangelism, in a form of the Christian religion which seems set to be transplanted wherever there is an expansion of this communications medium. This kind of religion is interesting in that it abjures the usual sense of community associated with the Christian religion. The evangelists will have a small community around them in their studio/churches but the bulk of their congregation and supporters, amounting to millions for each televised or broadcast service, will only be in touch by letter and their contribution cheque. The preacher is as remote from his congregation as the medieval Catholic priest was from his. In the case of the medieval Catholic priest it was his office and the action of the Mass which separated priest and laity, not physical distance. In the case of the television preacher it is physical distance in one sense, but the 'mystical' distance is almost as great as in the medieval church. Just as pop and rock stars become the high priests of twentieth-century culture, so the television preacher becomes a 'star' with all the ingredients of the pop-star mystique. The ingredients include a contrived setting, 'beautiful people', including the preacher himself, his voice, the music, and obvious wealth provided by the customers who seemingly like giving so that their 'idol' can become even more wealthy. This may not be immediately identifiable as clericalism, but that is what it is, and the notion of 'sacred person', though modified, persists.

7.3.3 This section refers mainly to the Anglican tradition which has its roots in the Reformation in the Church of England, which in so many ways was different from the other main Reformations. While the Church of England joined with others in eventually removing sacerdotalism it retained a strong sacramental spirit. The successive Books of Common Prayer testify to the attempt to maintain a strong liturgical base for the church. That motivation has ebbed and flowed over the centuries but never disappeared except during the English Revolution. The church retained the three orders of bishop, priest and deacon with relatively little controversy. Even the title 'Mass' was retained for a time.

In the ordination of a priest in the Anglican tradition it is clear that it is intended that the priest shall receive the gift of the Holy Spirit for specific tasks. The primary task in the order of the words of the ritual is the forgiving of sins. After that comes the faithful dispensing of the word of God and of the sacraments and the authority to preach the word of God. It seems obvious that, though sacerdotalism may have been rejected in respect of the action of the eucharist, it is firmly retained in the power of the keys. There is an element of ambiguity, however, for though interpreters such as Richard Hooker attempted to speak of the ministry in moderate terms, the whole ethos was reformatory and influenced by Calvinism. Yet the formularies are much more conservative and open to more than one interpretation.

After the Reformation, and in spite of the continental influence, there always remained in the Church of England (and as time went on in other parts of the Anglican communion) a significant High Church element. While this element stood for many things in the church, in the context of our present discussion the main things it stood for were a sacerdotal view of the priesthood with the restoration of the Mass. In the nineteenth century this and many other issues came to a head in the Church of England in the Oxford Movement (see *Encyclopedia*, pp.112–3). There was controversy over ritual and vestments but eventually the High Churchmen won their way, and today there are many individual parishes and whole areas of the Anglican Communion which have restored the sacrificial element to the eucharist and the work of the priest.

7.4 Women in the priesthood

It is in the context of the sacerdotalism of much of the Anglican Communion and of other Protestant churches that we can discuss the ordination of women to the full-time ministry. Considerable change has taken place in attitudes and policies relating to the ordination of women, and the extent of recent change is not reflected fully in all the set books for A213. With this point in mind, please now read *Encyclopedia*, pages 163–164.

An interesting feature of the controversy is that very often there is an alliance between the High and Low Church people or Evangelicals on the issue. Both wings take their stand on a conservative interpretation of the scriptures, holding that Jesus chose only males for his disciples. As with many other issues, religion is inherently conservative owing its allegiance to authoritative documents in its theology and morality. In this case modern views associated with the feminist movements are rejected because they conflict with holy writ but also because they challenge age-old dogmas and the church cannot be seen to have been wrong. A similar attitude is taken towards the movement within the Roman Catholic Church by priests who wish to overthrow canon law on the matter of the marriage of priests. Relating to the position of women, this kind of fundamentalism, at least in the case of the 'catholic' traditions, is also more than tinged with ancient taboos associated with menstruation and childbirth. In some traditions, including Anglican, and especially in India and Africa, women are often discouraged from coming to the altar rail to receive communion while menstruating. At the same time and after a long struggle, the first woman was ordained a priest in the Anglican Church in 1994.

You will return to the wider topic of women in religion in the second part of the course.

7.5 Clerics and the laity

In much of what we have discussed here it is clear that the churches have operated a system for many centuries and in all denominations where the clergy have played the role of dispensers of religious gifts, favours, power and grace, while the laity have been the recipients of the same. Even the word lay has come to stand for someone who is not proficient, who does not know whatever there is to be known. In the New Testament the word *laos* stands for the people of God, the whole people of God, not just the clergy. At the Reformation the attempt was made to recover this sense of the 'laos' of God, but it only partially succeeded. Indeed, it could be argued that after some initial success the position of the laity in many instances reverted to being what it was before the Reformation.

In this century an attempt has been made to restore the laity to their rightful place within the churches. The 'Church' in the different traditions has increasingly been redefined as clergy and people, not just the clergy. The laity are brought into discussions on all aspects of church policy. They are more and more visible in the ritual aspects of the churches, reading the scriptures publicly, administering the cup at communion. The reason for this change is partly on account of the problem of staffing the churches with reduced numbers of clergy, but also because of the rediscovery of 'the Church' in the biblical theology of this century. Indeed, it could be argued that for some the nature of the church has changed in that the gap between the sacred and the secular has deliberately been reduced, and one of the most important aspects of this democratization has been the reduction of the gap between clergy and laity. Dog collars are less in evidence and the laity dress much more casually when attending church rites. It is also evident in some cases in forms of speech where the clergy speak less of Thee and Thine in the liturgy and more of You and Yours, We and Us. The language that set them apart from the laity has been democratized. This is not a universal phenomenon and there are many who resist this change.

8 Worship and ritual

8.0.1 'Ritual' comes from the word rite, and this stands, usually, for a form of words that will be part of what is called worship. In this sense worship is the generic term for a certain form of religious activity and a rite will be a part of such worship. A rite may be expressed not only with words but also with ceremonial. In practice there is a tendency to use worship and ritual as interchangeable terms.

8.0.2 Worship is a general term derived from the Anglo-Saxon *weorthscipe* (worthship) meaning honour. The word is primarily used as a description of human activity in respect of the divine. In this sense God is to be the sole object of worship, which should be directed towards him alone. The worship of anything less than God, in a religious context, is deemed to be idolatry. In Jewish and Christian history the worship of any other God than 'the God of Abraham, Isaac and Jacob', or in the specifically Christian context, 'the God and Father of our Lord Jesus Christ', is also idolatry. The word stands for the general attitude required of the adherent of the Christian religion towards God and for the specific individual and corporate acts which are expressed ritually. The basic ingredients of Christian worship are thanksgiving and praise, but also included in worship is penance, including confession of sins, petitions (that is, prayers asking favours of God), and promises to observe God's holy laws. In the Christian religion worship may be formalized and ritualized using set forms, handed down over the centuries, and called liturgies (meaning 'the [religious] works of the people'), or worship may be informal, extempore, with no fixed forms. The former are generally found in the 'catholic' and moderate Protestant traditions, the latter in the radical Protestant traditions.

8.0.3 Ritual can be looked at theologically, sociologically or anthropologically. In the case of sociology or anthropology, the observance and performance of ritual is the prime example of religious social activity.

> Rituals are regular, repetitive, rule-determined patterns of symbolic behaviour, performed by one or more people, that utilize any or all of the following components: language, action, visual imagery, personification and characterization, specific objects imbued with meaning, and music. Rituals common to most cultures mark universally shared experiences – the new year, for example, occasions rituals in all cultures – or significant stages in the life-cycle, such as birth, puberty, marriage and death. Familiar religious rites comprise offerings of thanksgiving, petitions, sacrifices and adoration. In religious contexts rituals are generally agreed to serve as a bridge between the profane and sacred realms or, on a more individual level, between a believer and the deity.
>
> (Richardson and Bowden, eds, 1983, entry: 'Ritual')

Ritual may be very complex and elaborate. (For an example of this type see the programme 'Easter worship: the Greek liturgy' on video cassette 1.) Or it may be very simple, for example, a Pentecostal service which consists of extempore prayer, the reading of scripture, the singing of hymns and a sermon. In the latter context, and even more so in a meeting of the Society of Friends, the participants would probably assert that their worship is devoid of ritual. In the sense that there is very little if any ceremonial comparable to the Greek Liturgy this claim might be allowed. In the sense that the Pentecostal service and the Friends' meeting are 'regular, repetitive patterns of symbolic behaviour' they are ritualized events. It may be argued that they are not 'rule-determined patterns of symbolic behaviour' but observation would show that they are determined by unwritten and repeated rules of action. In this sense even the Friends' basic pattern of silence is ritualized silence.

8.1 Sacred space

The Christian religion, like all other religions, finds it necessary to set apart space on earth for the performance of rituals – spaces in which the devotees can meet God, be as it were in God's territory. There are various ways of looking at this subject. One way is to see sacred space as standing for the desire that the whole cosmos be sacred rather than being for the most part profane. The sacred is that which is set apart, made holy; the profane, strictly meaning 'before or outside the temple', is the other than the holy. Another way of looking at sacred space is the desire to 'bring down' heaven to earth, an idea we have seen formalized in the Orthodox church building.

Early meetings of the Christian community for worship were held in available space, that is private houses and synagogues. We have the record of a service of the breaking of bread on the first day of the week in an ordinary house in Troas in the New Testament. Paul preached at length so that a young man fell asleep and dropped out of an upstairs window (*Acts* 20:7–12). We also know that in Rome the early Christians, for fear of arrest and punishment, met for worship in the underground catacombs where they interred their dead. It was a couple of centuries after the resurrection of Christ before purpose-built buildings were used.

If we look at different examples of sacred space we will see that in different traditions the sense of the holy varies in intensity with regard to space. In Figure 1 (a–f) you will find outline drawings of six types of buildings which have developed during the history of the religion. Examine them carefully and note how the concept of sacred space varies with the individual tradition. Look at the general design and locate the areas designed to accommodate sacred action, and reflect on the religious attitude which might lie beneath the design. The shaded areas in the illustrations are an attempt to quantify the perception of the depth of sacredness in the different areas of the buildings of the different traditions. We will return to the Christian use of sacred space when we consider this topic in the second part of the course.

8.2 Sacred action and sacred time

Participating in sacred action creates sacred time, hours set apart for worship and ritual. In the Christian religion, as in the Jewish religion, it is history and the mythological interpretation of history, understood as the activity of God, which provides the basic context for the pursuit of sacred time and action. The larger mythological basis is the belief in the incarnation of God in his Son, Jesus Christ. This is a very powerful symbol of God's entry into and intervention in history. Within that larger context the last hours of the Son of God on earth provide the mythological structure of the sacred action and the boundaries of sacred time. Before the New Testament church ran into difficulties with the Jewish authorities the followers of Jesus obviously continued their religious practice within the sacred parameters of the Jewish faith. We are told that two of his followers, Peter and John, went to the temple in Jerusalem 'at the hour of prayer' (*Acts* 3:1). This story implies that this was an habitual act on their part. In other words the earliest followers of Jesus, strictly speaking before they became Christians, followed the practice of their leader in attending worship in the

Basilica type

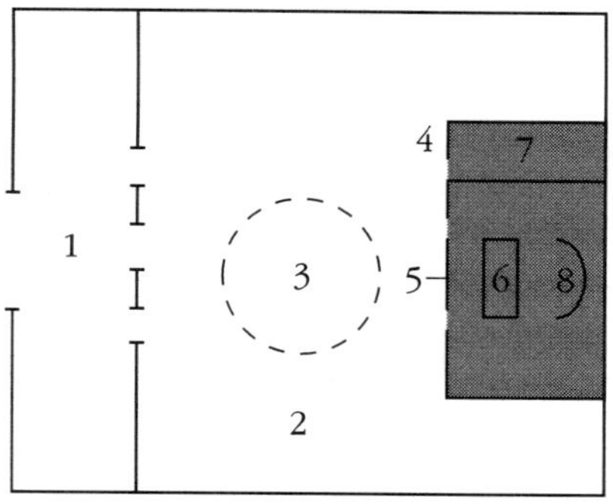

A

1 Narthex – porch for preparation
2 Nave – no seating; congregation stands, walks
3 Dome above, painted with Christ as ruler
4 Iconostasis – screen covered with icons
5 Central door – opened during service
6 Altar
7 Chapel for preparation of bread and wine
8 Bishop's seat in semi-circular 'apse'

Cruciform type

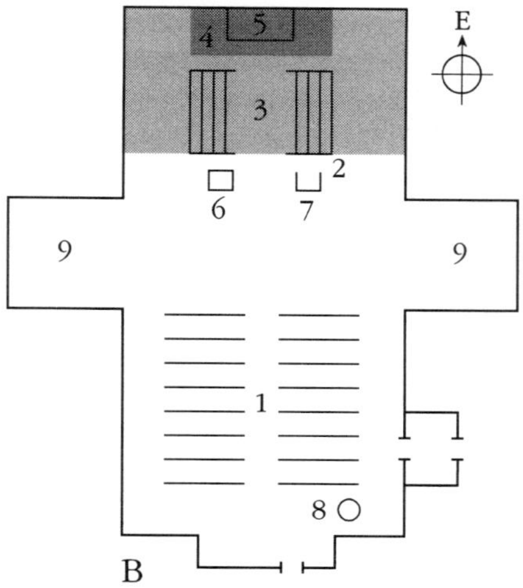

B

1 Nave – seated congregation
2 Screen (in older churches) – open door
3 Choir (where service is led)
4 Sanctuary (railed)
5 Altar table
6 Pulpit (for preaching)
7 Lectern (for reading Scriptures)
8 Font (for baptism)
9 Transepts (side chapels)

Meeting-house type

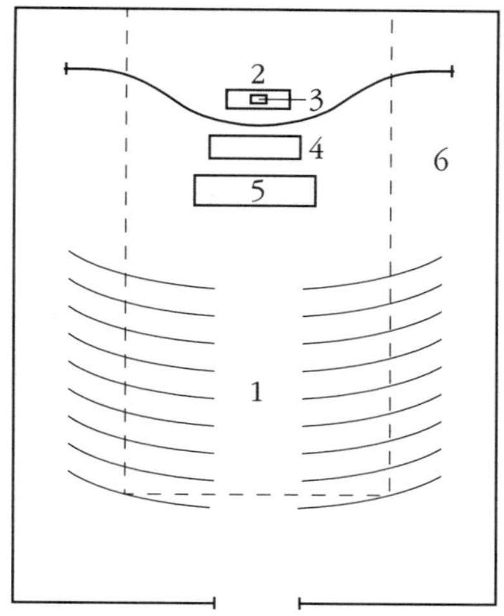

C

1 Congregation seated
2 Pulpit (where service is led)
3 Bible (open for service)
4 Communion table (no rails)
5 Baptistery in Baptist tradition (covered when not in use)
6 Balcony (occasionally for choir)

Basle Cathedral, Calvinistic Presbyterian

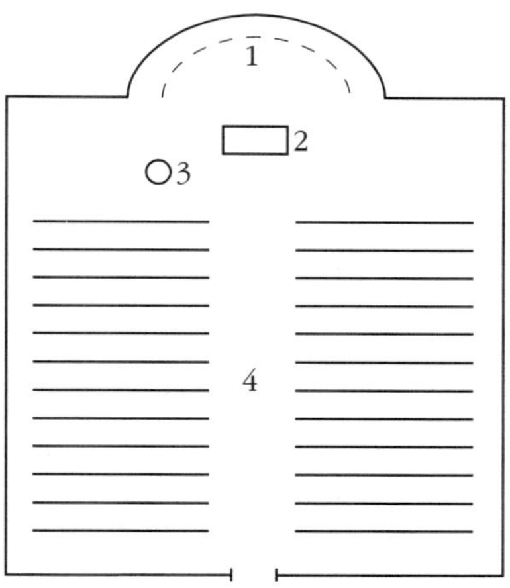

D

1 Seating for Presbyters
2 Table
3 Font
4 Congregation seated

Dual-purpose parish church (Anglican)

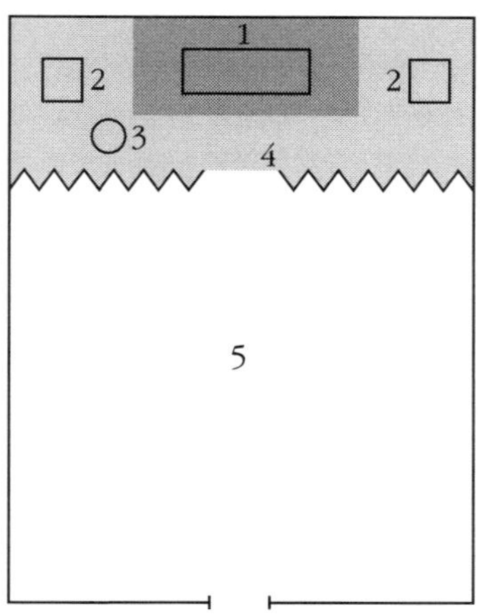

E

1 Altar table
2 Pulpitum
3 Font (moveable)
4 Moveable partition
5 Adaptable space

American-style Evangelistic Meeting place

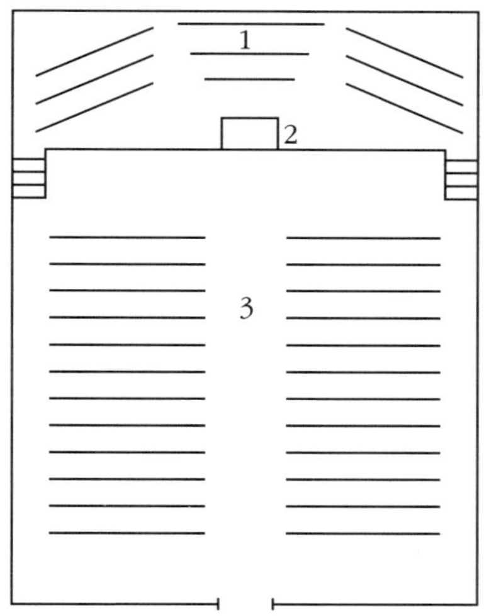

F

1 Choir seating
2 Lectern
3 Congregation seated

Figure 1 Arrangements of sacred space

temple and in the synagogue. Later the rudimentary Christian organization adopted its own arrangement of rituals. This was partly because of conflict with the Jewish authorities (Peter and John were arrested on the visit referred to above for healing a person and for preaching about Jesus), partly because they would have needed some distinctive way of celebrating their belief in the efficacy of the teaching, death and resurrection of their leader. The first day of the week became their main day of worship rather than the seventh, the former being the day of resurrection (*Acts* 20:7). It is clearly a move to make present again and again that sacred time when their saviour rose from the dead. So sacred time is established but how is it to be actualized? In half the Christian religion, the half that will subsequently be referred to as 'high-sacramental', it is actualized in the eucharist.

The action arises from an activity of their leader in an event which began the final phase of his short life. For a more detailed discussion of the rite's antecedents and its place in early Christianity, see section 4.2. It is known as the eucharist (stressing the words of *thanksgiving* used), or Holy Communion (stressing the sharing in fellowship), or Mass (from the words of dismissal at the end of the rite in the Latin form), or Lord's Supper (stressing the belief in the presence of the risen Lord Jesus). In addition to the bread and wine, the main ritual objects, the chalice and paten (cup and plate), which contain the elements, are treated as ritual implements, with a great deal of reverence attaching to them. In addition there is a cultic object which is closely associated with location of the eucharist, a reproduction of a cross or a crucifix. Either form is a remembrance of the death that took place on it. The crucifix emphasizes the agony and suffering of Jesus, the empty cross his resurrection. There will be a book containing the liturgy, in the Roman tradition called a missal, which is treated with reverence, the page from which the gospel is read will often be kissed by the celebrant, but there will be no Bible. That will be found on a lectern in a position which is outside the main ritual area.

One of the key words in the belief in the inauguration of the rite and in its actual performance is the word 'remembrance'. We find a similar use of the idea of remembrance in Sikhism and Judaism. *Nam simaran* in Sikhism means recalling or bringing to remembrance the name of God. In Judaism this element of bringing to remembrance is associated with *Pesach*, in which the deliverance from slavery in Egypt is brought to mind. But it is present in virtually every religious context very often through the re-enactment of some historical or primeval myth, especially myths of origin. In this sense the eucharist is the ritualization of the myth of the origin of the Christian religion. The ritual is not just remembering. In all these religious contexts remembering means bringing the past into the present, making effective again that original mythological event and its power. To be sure, the life and death of Jesus is a fairly incontrovertible historical fact. However its treatment in doctrine and in ritual action moves beyond raw facts to interpret his brutal execution as the occasion for the salvation of the world. In every celebration of the ritual participants are caught up in the drama of the event recalled: 'On the same night that he was betrayed he took bread ... wine ... gave thanks ('eucharist-ed') and gave it ...'; and the power of the event is transmitted, whatever the precise doctrinal explanation given within the individual Christian tradition. In the high sacramental traditions certain festivals are special occasions for the celebration of the eucharist. Festivals are divided into two main categories: those associated with the life story of Jesus Christ, including feast days related to his mother, the Blessed Virgin Mary; and those associated with the 'heroes and heroines' of the faith, the saints both from New Testament and from later times. Christmas and Easter are prominent among the festivals associated with Jesus, while the rest often depend on devotions to particular local or universal saints, such as the massive celebration on the feast of St James in Santiago de Compostela in northern Spain.

The worship discussed above and its association with the kind of cultic religious patterns described is typical of the 'high sacramental' type of the Christian religion. In contrast there is a 'low sacramental' type. At this point we should be aware of some dispute, for there are those who would argue that there are forms of the Christian religion which show no sacramental awareness at all. Reference can be made to the evangelical television-studio type of Christianity which seems devoid of all ceremony and ceremonial or ritual appurtenances and is more akin to 'show biz'. If the term sacrament is narrowly defined, in terms of the investing of material things with divine power, or material things being vehicles of divine power in a restricted sense, then this type of personalized religion is not sacramental. In these units, however, any object, person, event or situation which is perceived as occasioning an encounter with the divine, is to be understood as sacramental. Therefore we can speak of 'low sacramental' type religion which will include a range of ritual and worship patterns with the moderate Protestant at one end and the radical, even extreme individualized Protestant at the other.

The 'low sacramental' nature of the major Protestant denominations is more complicated than the 'high sacramental' traditions. There are those in the Protestant traditions who take a 'high' view of worship, with emphasis on the regular celebration of the Lord's Supper (the term 'eucharist' is seldom used in this context). On the other hand what was once the regular pattern caricatured in some quarters as 'the Nonconformist sandwich' – the layers of the sandwich being a hymn, prayer, hymn, scripture reading, hymn, sermon, hymn, a pattern similar to synagogue worship – has given way to a more ordered liturgical pattern in many denominations. Lutheran and Presbyterian traditions have, generally, always had a fairly conventional, ordered liturgical life. The radical Protestant traditions, until fairly recently, abjured all kinds of ordered liturgical practice. The emphasis was always on the inspired, extempore form of worship. The accent was always verbal rather than ritual, using the term ritual in its strictest sense. What happened generally turned out to be a ritualized verbalism. More recently, under the influence of a liturgical revival in all the major traditions and through the influence of contacts made within the ecumenical movement, even more radical churches have admitted service books with set prayers and forms of worship. This movement is by no means universal in these traditions and there is fierce resistance from the more radical traditionalists in these denominations.

In spite of these internal complications in the 'low sacramental' area of the Christian religion and the growth of pre-arranged forms of worship, the spirit of this worship is to a certain extent reflected in the Nonconformist sandwich. There is a strong emphasis on the reading of scripture, on preaching the word of God and on hymn singing. Hymn singing especially is a feature of the low sacramental traditions. These hymns, composed by some of the leading Christians of their time, including Martin Luther and Charles Wesley, have become an enormous storehouse of devotion. There is no aspect of the Christian life which is not reflected in the hymnody of the low sacramental traditions. They have replaced the accent in the older liturgies on the Book of Psalms and other canticles, like the Magnificat, the song sung by Mary on the occasion of her visit to Elizabeth, mother of John the Baptist (*Luke* 1:46–55). In some low sacramental traditions like the Church of Scotland, metrical psalms have continued to be used extensively. In some 'high sacramental' traditions the singing of these hymns has also become a major feature. The singing of hymns was legalized in the Church of England in 1820. The Second Vatican Council, in sanctioning the use of the vernacular in the Mass and congregational hymn singing, ratified practices already followed in certain quarters of the Roman Catholic Church. The practice of repeatedly singing well-known hymns, so that they are memorized by many devotees, gives a stability and continuity to the ongoing life of the churches. Western missionary churches in non-western cultures have often shown their insensitivity to local culture in the adoption, not only of the words of these hymns, but also their tunes. There are significant exceptions such as in the church in Maharashtra, India, where the conversion of a leading Marathi poet led to a marvellous collection of hymns in the Indian *bhakti* (devotional) tradition, and in the vernacular lyrics sung in the churches of Nigeria and Ghana.

Whereas the Bible, as a physical object, is absent from the main form of worship in the high sacramental traditions (though a selection of its contents will be included in the liturgical book), in the low sacramental traditions the Bible, both as that which contains the inspired word and as the main cultic object, has a central and unchallenged place. We have seen something of the debate over its precise status as 'the word of God'; here we see it as the effective cultic object, placed in a prominent position, open physically and symbolically, and replacing the Host and the ritual implements of the eucharist as the expression of the talismanic tendency. In one sense it may be wrong to label the traditions we are now discussing as low sacramental because the Bible, in these traditions, very often represents a sacramental intensity which is unparalleled even in the most sacerdotalist, pre-Reformation environment. Christians of other traditions often dub those who respond to the Bible in this intensely sacramental, even talismanic, way as Bibliolaters, that is, people who have substituted the book for an idol. In certain Evangelical traditions the material book, the Bible, becomes a form of ritual implement. Whatever the precise nature of the tradition the exegesis of a text from the Bible is the basic form of preaching – the sermon being the high point of the ritualized sequence.

The third element in the 'sandwich' is prayer which, apart from those sections of the low sacramental traditions who have adopted service books, is extempore. It is held to be the product of religious experience. No doubt the prayers of the ancient liturgies are also products of religious experience, a 'treasury of devotion' as they are sometimes called, but in the traditions under consideration it is claimed that the experience is immediate. Such a prayer in a regular 'nonconformist' service will often last several minutes with the prayer moving from thanksgiving, through penitence and petition, to dedication to God's service. The language will be laced with familiar phrases, including phrases from the Bible. Often the language includes reminding God what kind of a being he is, merciful, gracious, bountiful; then will follow the petitions. The whole ethos of the prayer is different from the balanced phrases and literary structure of ancient liturgies. Here the prayer speaks to someone with whom he or she is familiar, like speaking to a friend as opposed to speaking to a potentate. The style is generally more chatty, less formal, more vernacular in vocabulary, less archaic in construction. The theology in some ways is the same as found in the traditional liturgies but it is the theology of a more immanent, less transcendent deity. It is noticeable that much of the liturgical revision of recent times, certainly in the Church of England and in the Roman Catholic Church, has tended to move closer to the theological position of the low sacramental traditions in language and style. With the removal of archaic language the vernacular is more prominent and the ethos of worship is democratized and personalized. It is also sometimes said, however, that the gap between sacred and profane is thereby reduced, and the liturgy made more ordinary and less mysterious.

8.3 Life-cycle rites

Life-cycle rites, or rites of passage, are a prominent feature of every religious tradition. In the Christian religion there are fewer such rites than in many other religions and the pattern differs between Christian traditions. In some traditions there are birth, puberty, marriage and funeral rites. In others birth and puberty rites may vary. In the Orthodox traditions there is no puberty rite, while in some of the radical Protestant traditions there is no birth rite. There are various views of the purpose of these rites. One of the most commonly held is that the rites give a stable structure to society. The new individual within the society is welcomed into that society and will eventually learn of that entry into the society, either by mementoes of the occasion or by the presence of elders who have a particular responsibility for aspects of the young one's growth to full membership of the group. In puberty young persons, in ritual, take on their own responsibilities as adult members of the group. The next stage is the public acknowledgement in ritual of the taking of a spouse and the support that is offered to the new family unit. Finally with the death of a member of the group rituals safeguard the entry of the deceased into whatever changed form of life is believed in, and assist those left behind to cope with the grief of losing one of their dear relations.

Baptism, which is a form of initiation in the Christian religion, is surrounded by theological controversy, as we have seen in 4.1 above. From the standpoint of life-cycle rites the matter takes on a different perspective. Such a cycle of rites pre-dates the events discussed in 4.1. We are therefore faced with the problem of which rite is the initiation rite. Theologically one must maintain that baptism is the initiation rite. But generally speaking initiation rites are associated with puberty. Compare bar mitzvah in Judaism (Units 1–2 section 8.4.2) and the thread ceremony in Hinduism (*Encyclopedia* p.240).

According to some 'catholic' beliefs, baptism is the antidote to the effects of original sin. Without the antidote the individual is lost forever in hell or limbo. So baptism is administered as soon as is practical and very quickly if there is an emergency. Baptism is also administered to infants in moderate Protestant traditions but without the theology associated with the 'catholic' traditions. In the Orthodox traditions, at the time of baptism the infant is also chrismated, that is, anointed with the holy oil. This practice anticipates what is left to a later stage of life in the other 'catholic' and moderate Protestant traditions. The chrismation is an act of 'confirmation' and immediately after baptism and chrismation in the Orthodox traditions an infant may be offered Holy Communion in the form of bread, dipped in wine, and administered with a spoon. In all other traditions where infant baptism is administered there will be an act of confirmation and acceptance into adult membership around the age of puberty. The person so confirmed or accepted is thereafter accepted at the table during the Lord's supper. In the Roman tradition first communion generally precedes confirmation by some years. In those traditions in which it occurs 'confirmation' is clearly a puberty rite, whatever the theology claimed for it. This is not to suggest, however, that confirmation never takes place at times other than puberty – it is by no means uncommon for people to be confirmed at a much later stage in their life. (See section 4.1.2 above.)

There is disagreement between different traditions and within the Anglican tradition as to whether confirmation is a sacrament or not. At the Reformation the Protestants reaffirmed that there were only two sacraments of the church, namely those commanded by Christ, baptism and eucharist. The Church of England retained rituals other than these two dominical sacraments (that is, instituted by Jesus, from the Latin 'dominus' meaning

'Lord') but referred to them as 'commonly called sacraments'. The other contentious rites are confirmation, marriage, penance (including absolution), ordination to the ministry and extreme unction, commonly referred to as 'the last rites'. The argument surrounds the question as to whether Christ commanded them and whether they conform to the usual structure of a sacrament in having 'an outward and visible sign' of 'an inward and invisible grace'. In baptism and the eucharist the signs are material and visible and become symbols by their special use in a special context. In some of the other rites the signs are the laying on of hands, the use of oil in extreme unction, and the exchanging of vows in marriage. The theological basis of calling them sacraments is a matter of debate and continues to be so. The recognition of all the rites, and not only the life-cycle rites, as ritualized events of the affirmation of individual or group purposes, the continuation of race through marriage, the removal of guilt through penance and absolution, the setting apart of sacred persons in ordination, the (full) initiation of the individual into group activity in confirmation (or adult baptism in the radical Protestant traditions), and the preparation for death in extreme unction, is much clearer and can be seen to be universal religious elements in the Christian religion.

9 Moral theology and Christian ethics

9.0.1 In every religion, as in all social systems, there is some provision for regulating the life of the community. Religious regulations often derive their legitimacy from a claim that they have been received through revelation. The regulations are understood as sacred law and may be written or oral. They may apply over a whole religion or there may be a general code with local or sub-group regulations. Again, as with all social systems, such regulations will be so formulated and developed within the tradition that there is the maximum encouragement to observe the regulations, and a range of sanctions which can be applied against those who infringe them. There are various forms of sanction, the most extreme being the exclusion of the offender from membership of the community. The decision to impose sanctions will be vested in someone or some body with the authority to do so, and the exercise of such authority will often be seen as the exercise of divine sanction. This way of putting things stresses the social control aspect of religion, reflecting the positive purpose towards which such regulation is directed. In Christian thought, ethics have been understood as oriented towards an ultimate end, the 'Good', identified in Christian tradition with the kingdom of God. Therefore, negative prohibitions need to be understood in terms of this overall positive context of seeking the fulfilment of God's reign on earth.

According to the influential sociologist Max Weber (1869–1920), the formulation of a code of behaviour occurs quite late in the formulation of a new religious group or organization associated with a charismatic leader. The ecstatic community does not need rules, for two reasons. First, it is enough to listen to the charismatic leader, to absorb his or her attitudes. Secondly, the movement surrounding the leader will be essentially an unorganized, world-denying movement with none of the complications which most social groups face in this world. It is only in the later stages of the leader's life, or after the leader is removed from the scene, that the complications of group living become apparent. Gradually the need for rules and regulations grows and produces an embryonic code which will eventually take on the structure of the kind of bureaucracy which the leader refused to accept in the initial charismatic moment. Some have seen this kind of pattern in the development of the Christian religion. However, it needs to be applied with caution. Although Jesus rejected rigid interpretation of Jewish law, he presupposed the complex moral and regulatory structure of Torah and much of the tradition that had developed around it.

The terms 'moral theology' and 'Christian ethics' used in the title of this section may, at first, appear to be interchangeable and therefore unnecessary. Why not moral theology *or* Christian ethics – why both? Broadly speaking the term 'moral theology' is used by the 'catholic' traditions and the term 'Christian ethics' by the Protestant traditions. Orthodox traditions fall outside this division.

James M. Gustafson (1978) has suggested that one difference between the Roman Catholic and the Protestant positions is that moral theology in the Roman tradition developed 'in the service of the priestly role in the sacrament of penance'. Thus, in determining the moral guilt of the penitent through confession, a juridical role is exercised by the priest which is absent in the Protestant traditions. Gustafson notes that the Anglican tradition has come close at times to the understanding of morality and law found in the Roman tradition. A large body of moral theology has been built up in the history of the Roman Catholic Church and some of its leading theologians, such as Thomas Aquinas, have included within their work extensive judgements on the nature and range of sins which must be dealt with within the penitential system. In addition to the penitential factor in the Roman tradition there is the 'magisterial' or teaching authority of the Church. Roman Catholicism recognizes three sources of theological authority: scripture, tradition (each authorized and interpreted by the magisterium), and reason. Consequently, the Catholic Church, mainly through the Pope as the head of the 'magisterium', the authoritative body of bishops, claims the right to prescribe what it considers to be correct behaviour in a whole range of moral matters ranging from the conduct of affairs of state down to contraception.

By contrast, in Protestantism there is a lack of central sources equivalent to the Roman Catholic magisterium to regulate the interpretation of scripture and tradition. This has led to a greater range of opinions about ethical matters, and to a greater stress on scripture in some denominations (conservative and fundamentalist), and on reason and conscience in some other denominations (liberal). This description of Protestantism, however, should distinguish between freedom and licence to do just what one will. There is within Protestantism a consensus on certain aspects of behaviour. Some denominations and groups have substantial disciplinary practices. Discipline can only be exercised in Protestantism, however, against those sins, or moral misdemeanours, which manifest themselves publicly. In the absence of a confessional system, within which the secrets of the heart are – theoretically at least – revealed to the confessor, disciplinary action can only be taken against breaches of the ethical code which become public or community knowledge. For example, historically women who conceive out of wedlock have traditionally been the most likely to suffer discipline. Action against the male partner in such liaisons has been much less frequent. But this can also be seen as part of a wider pattern of discrimination within religions. This issue will be discussed more fully in the set text *Women in Religion* and in the related study guide.

9.1 The sources of moral/ethical judgement

There are two ways of looking at the basis of moral judgement in the Christian religion. The two aspects relate to the dual background of the religion based as it is on the life, death and resurrection of Jesus, but also as we have already seen on the Judaic background to that life. Thus the Christian religion accepts the basic demands of the Jewish Torah as exemplified by the Decalogue or The Ten Commandments (see *Reader* 1.1.3). The rest of Torah, the written Torah, the Christian Old Testament, has the status of 'the Word of God' for Christians as well as Jews, though it is not always clear to what extent Christians are expected to conform to the larger Torah. We have seen that the question of authority of Torah is a problem for Jews (see Units 1–2 section 1.7). How much more is it a problem for Christians? There are those on the extreme conservative wing of the religion who claim to accept as authoritative everything that is contained in Torah because it is a direct revelation from God. Whether they are able to conform to this belief in practice in all its details is another matter. The problem for Christians as a whole, however, is the relationship between what Jesus, and for that matter what the apostle Paul, said, and the revelation contained in the Old Testament.

Exercise

Please read 'The Sermon on the Mount' in *Reader* 2.3, as far as '... and your Father who sees in secret will reward you'. Note what Jesus says about the law and compare what he says about different rules and laws with

Reader 1.1.3. Have this question in mind: does Jesus agree with the Old Testament law (Torah), or is he modifying the law, or is he over-ruling the law? (See also section 2.3.7 above.)

Discussion

At first Jesus appears to be upholding the law. Not an iota or dot (references to the pointing in the Hebrew script, the written Torah) will be set aside 'until all is accomplished'. Whoever merely 'relaxes' one of the least of the commandments will be the least in the kingdom of heaven. (I think we can assume that what is to be accomplished is the inauguration of the kingdom of heaven, or the kingdom of God.) Then follows a series of references to the Torah, each prefaced with a similar formula, 'You have heard it said ... But I say to you ...'. What follows, at first, is a modification of the ancient law, a modification that is more demanding. It is not enough to refrain from murder; you must not even lose your temper with the other person. It is not enough to refrain from adultery; you must not, at least men must not, look lustfully at a woman, for the look itself is adultery. The law on divorce is to be tightened up and the custom of swearing by something, not merely swearing falsely, is to be abolished. Now it could be argued that these strictures are in tune with the old laws, going to the heart of what the old laws are really about. But the next two statements appear to be different.

The first deals with the old law, not original to Judaism, the *lex talionis*, the law of retaliation. (See the Jewish interpretation of this law in Units 1–2 section 1.6.3.) The second deals with the law by which different responses are prescribed for neighbours and enemies. In both instances Jesus appears to be over-ruling the old law, not just modifying it. Retaliation is out, non-resistance to violence is in. Hating enemies is out, loving even enemies is in. He goes on to charge that his followers should be perfect 'as your heavenly Father is perfect'. The old law which was built on a number of accommodations, not only with neighbours but also, to be fair, with enemies, does appear to be superseded by a new ethics, the ethics of the kingdom of heaven. Which brings us back to the beginning of the passage dealing with the old law. Not a jot or dot will pass away until the kingdom of heaven is accomplished – that appears to be the distinction. There is law for existence this side of the kingdom and a law which operates within the kingdom. Now let us turn to what the apostle Paul has to say.

9.2 The ethics of Paul

The inauguration of the kingdom of God does not feature prominently in Paul's writings, but that which the kingdom stands for in the teaching of Jesus does. It is generally referred to as 'the coming' of Jesus at the end of this age or aeon. It is the *parousia* of Jesus. Just as the coming of the kingdom is a key to the ethics of Jesus, so is the coming of Jesus a key to the ethics of Paul. The law and what supersedes the law also features in the teaching of Paul, and we get the same tension between the law and its age, and the new age which is the age of love and grace. (It should be made clear that this is a Christian interpretation of law, one that Jews would not agree with.) In Paul there is also a tension between salvation by observing the law (or works) and salvation by faith (or grace). Paul does not advocate the shedding of the old law. When he raises the question of the priority of faith he asks: 'Do we then overthrow the law by this faith? By no means! On the contrary, we uphold the law' (*Romans* 3:31). Yet he goes on to say: 'My brethren, you have died to the law through the body of Christ, so that you may belong to another, to him who has been raised from the dead in order that we may bear fruit for God'. On the basis of this statement he asks if the law is therefore sin? His answer is: 'By no means! Yet, if it had not been for the law, I should have not known sin. I should have not known what it is to covet if the law had not said, "You shall not covet".' In a perverse way this knowledge makes him sinful and causes his spiritual death. However that death is not due to the law but to sin. The law itself, the commandment itself, is 'holy and just and good'. This is a very complex issue, probably because Paul was a good Jew and still believed that the Torah was a revelation and therefore could not be abrogated easily. The distinction he wants to make is that the law is good. It acts like a 'tutor' until a person finds Christ. It takes care of the individual acts that force decisions upon us day by day, but in the great matter of our eternal salvation then it is commitment to Christ in response to his grace that ensures salvation. We are justified, made right with God, not by works but by grace through faith. (See *Reader* 2.5.1.) There are rules to be observed, rules to do with the family and neighbours and the state, and we will look at these presently, but the primary factor is 'the love of God in Christ Jesus our Lord'.

9.3 Law and grace

It is through the writing of Paul that one of the basic factors in any moral decision making has come down to us. It is the tension that exists between law and grace. Although it is quite clear in the New Testament that the basis of life in the new dispensation is the grace of God made present through Jesus and faith in Jesus, nevertheless in the real world the need for rule and definition demands that as yet the law cannot be completely abrogated. The Christian religion demands that Christians live towards grace while remaining within the purview of the law. The good life is the maintenance of a balance between law and grace. One can liken it to the construction of a suspension bridge. The physical chasm, which is the gap between demand and decision in the moral sense, is bridged by a structure which depends for its stability on the equal opposing tensions exerted at each end. If too much tension is exerted at one end, or if the tension at one end is diminished, then the structure collapses. In the same way, moral decision making in Christian terms is the maintenance of a balance between the tendency to oppression and heteronomy (being subject to the power of others, especially of an elite hierarchy), and the tendency to anarchy and autonomy (fulfilling one's own interests and ignoring the interests of the whole group). The suspension-bridge model probably reflects reality in Christian morals at their best, but is probably defective in describing the true Christian aim in that there should be a balance of attraction towards grace over law.

Another emphasis in Christian morals is that on love. When asked which was the primary commandment Jesus answered: 'you shall love the Lord your God with all your heart ... The second is this, You shall love your neighbour as yourself.' He was quoting from the Hebrew Bible, and it is as well to be reminded that most, if not all, he taught is either to be found in that Bible or is paralleled in the teaching of the rabbis. Here, however, Jesus is stressing the primacy of love, *agapé*. In some forms of Christian ethics, especially in this century, there has been an emphasis on 'love ethics' as opposed to the traditional 'command ethics'. This is the case among those who propose 'situation ethics', meaning that moral decisions should be made in the light of the immediate situation and on the basis that the only absolute is love.

This kind of attack on 'command ethics' has to be tempered by the way in which command ethics, especially in the Roman tradition, have been employed. Here we have the use of 'casuistry'. Casuistry has always had a bad press because it seems as if the aim is to be compromising and to avoid harsh or unpopular decisions. In fact casuistry refers to the practice of applying the absolute or general moral law to particular *cases* (casuistry from the Latin *casus*, or case). In this way the particular circumstances are taken into account in advising on a moral decision.

9.4 Moral issues: selected examples

There are many moral issues which we could look at but there is not the space. In the whole of moral theology one can find the treatment of virtually any human activity in terms of what is prescribed and proscribed. Here we will deal only with a few issues which are fairly common and which most of us may be concerned with at some time or other. Further discussion of Christian moral decision making is to be found in the set book *Making Moral Decisions* and in the related study guide and audio cassette. You will make a close study of these in the second part of the course.

9.4.1 The Christian and war

This topic, as indeed are the others to be studied here, is related to the larger subject of the relation between the Christian religion and the state. You will find a treatment of that subject as it affects the Orthodox traditions in *Encyclopedia*, pages 92 to 93, and certain aspects of the same subject as it relates to Protestantism in *Encyclopedia*, pages 115 to 120.

Throughout the history of the Christian religion there has been a vital strain of people who have opposed violence in any form, especially war, appealing to a cardinal injunction in the Sermon on the Mount, namely to love one's enemies (*Reader* 2.3). They have adopted a pacifist stance with its consequent disfavour. The alliances with the state which have formed the normal attitude of the churches towards the state, however, have resulted in the churches at least acquiescing in war and often blessing the conduct of it. While this is true it must always be said that the churches at their best have considered war to be a problematic issue and have worked towards the limiting of wars and their effects. One of the ways in which this has been done is in the formulation of the doctrine of the 'just war'. We should distinguish between this doctrine and the notion of 'holy wars', most of which seem to have been based on anything but the notion of a just war. The doctrine of the just war developed over a period of time and was an attempt to deal with something which was considered to be essentially evil. The doctrine was elaborated by Thomas Aquinas and stated as follows:

(a) War must be waged by a constituted authority.

(b) The cause for which it is fought must be just.

(c) There must be the intention of establishing good or rectifying evil.

A fourth clause was added later:

(d) The war must be waged by proper means.

It should be obvious that such a code belongs to an age which probably came to an end with World War I, certainly with World War II. The fourth clause probably was broken in World War I when the war was fought on the basis of which side would have the most men left after the slaughter had exhausted itself. It was broken in World War II long before Hiroshima and Nagasaki with the bombing of Coventry and Dresden. The third clause would disappear in a mushroom cloud if a total nuclear war broke out since there would be nothing left in which good could be established.

The code had as one of its basic presuppositions the separation of 'military' and 'civilian' targets. This presupposition has become impossible to sustain under the conditions of modern warfare because of the blurring of the distinctions between military and civilian. Nowadays Christian moralists are faced with very real problems in respect of war and there seems to be very little, if anything, to separate the Christian from the secularist on the virtues or otherwise of nuclear defence. Except for the pacifists, the pros and the antis employ many of the same arguments as the secularists and therefore talk of a new version of the just war, namely the 'limited war'. But Christians can still make a significant contribution to the ongoing debate in terms of the critique of nationalism as state idolatry, the unity of humanity as created by God, and the stewardship of creation as ordained by God. Some of the most distinctive contributions to discussion of Christian ethics and state violence have been made by proponents of 'liberation theology' in Latin America and elsewhere (see *Reader* 2.20, 2.23 and 2.25).

9.4.2 Marriage and divorce

The scriptural source of authority on the moral issues related to marriage and divorce has played quite an important part over the centuries. One of the key texts is one you have read already, the paragraph relating to divorce in 'The Sermon on the Mount' in *Reader* 2.3. First, however, we should look at marriage itself.

Mark 10:1–9 also takes up the Mosaic permission to divorce in response to a question from his adversaries. According to *Deuteronomy* 24:1, a man may divorce his wife if 'she finds no favour in his eyes because he has found some indecency in her' and write her 'a bill of divorce'. The view of Jesus is that Moses, who he held to be the author of *Deuteronomy*, only allowed this for his adversaries' 'hardness of heart' but that 'from the beginning it was not so'. 'From the beginning' is a reference to the story of the beginning of the race in *Genesis* 2, which states that 'a man leaves his father and his mother and cleaves to his wife, and they become one flesh'. This fact is made into a rule, the 'one flesh rule', which leads, according to Jesus and to Paul, to the indissolubility of the marriage union. Indeed, for Paul the same applies if the union is with a prostitute. It is this 'one flesh rule' which is behind the law on the completion of the marriage contract by consummation in the sexual act, and the statement by Jesus, 'What therefore God has joined together, let not man put asunder' (*Mark* 10:9). This last statement has been the basis of the Christian attitude towards marriage throughout the history of the religion. It is the position from which all moral discussion of marriage proceeds. It is reinforced by the further positive view of marriage, possibly Paul's, that the union between man and woman is analogous to the union between Christ and his church (*Ephesians* 5:21–23). In a passage which is definitely Paul's he does offer a positive view of the equal sharing of conjugal rights for those who marry in order to avoid temptation or to avoid being burned up with passion! (*1 Corinthians* 7). It is argued, with some justification, that while the views of Jesus or Paul may not be in tune with a modern view of male/female relations, nevertheless their attitude towards women as women in their own time was enlightened. Paul's views may have been too tied to the conventions of his time so that women were seen to play a subordinate role in society, but in terms of their status in the pattern of salvation there was no equivocation. It must be remembered also that his views on marriage were conditioned by his expectations that things were coming to an end. That is why he thought 'that in view of the impending distress it is well for a person to remain as he is', if unmarried then to remain unmarried, if married then not to seek to be free. His view that marriage was an antidote to temptation and the flames of passion did persist and was a feature of the reasons for marriage until fairly recently in some marriage services.

In western Christianity the traditional view is that marriage is a sacrament, though there has been some debate on this within the Anglican tradition. In the western traditions it was claimed that marriage had three purposes. They were, first, 'the procreation of children, to be brought up in the fear and nurture of the Lord'; secondly, 'for a remedy against sin, and to avoid fornication'; and thirdly, 'for the mutual society, help and comfort, that the one ought to have of the other' (*Book of Common Prayer*). This view is a reflection of Roman canon law. It is noticeable that the purposes concentrate on sexual relations within marriage and the notion of interpersonal relationships comes third and the expression of such relationship is not linked with the sexual relationship. In this century there has been a greater awareness in the 'catholic' traditions of the role that sexual relations play in the total relationship. Recent Anglican marriage services put the mutual help and comfort first and a more positive attitude towards the sexual act is adopted. In the Roman tradition, the Second Vatican Council spoke of marriage as 'the primary form of interpersonal communion'. Love pervades the whole of married life, it was said, and 'is uniquely expressed and perfected through the marital act'.

In Luther's view marriage was not a sacrament. As something belonging essentially to the realm of creation rather than redemption, marriage is governed by natural law, understood as God's law, and not by the gospel. This view was also reflected in the *Book of Common Prayer*, which said that marriage was 'instituted of God in the time of man's innocence'. As such Luther believed that it was a social protection against sin rather than a channel of sanctifying grace. Marriage was one of the divine ordinances rooted in the creative will of God.

It has to be recognized throughout the Christian religion that marriages do sometimes fail. In all traditions the intention in solemnizing marriage is that the union is for life in accordance with the words of Jesus as recorded in the gospels. However in the face of reality different traditions adopt various attitudes to divorce, or rather to the possibility of remarriage of divorcees. Divorced persons may or may not face temporary discipline in some traditions. Remarried divorcees often face much tougher forms of discipline. In the Anglican tradition, for instance, such a person will normally be barred from the communion table, but after a period when their 'sincerity' is proved they may be restored to communicant status again. In the Roman tradition the very act of divorce is considered an impossibility and anyone remarrying after divorce will be considered to be in the state of adultery while the first spouse remains alive. The Roman tradition does permit the annulment of a marriage if the grounds can be argued and a judgement found in favour of such annulment. Increasingly such a procedure is being viewed by Roman Catholics as a scandal, since the judicial procedure is prohibitively expensive and therefore restricted to a wealthy minority, and the length of time taken to arrive at a decision leaves couples in a state of genuine suffering. In some Protestant traditions the view is taken that while divorce is unwelcome and contrary to the Christian view of marriage, nevertheless, there are cases of irretrievable breakdown which can cause agony to otherwise faithful Christians. The compassionate line to take, therefore, is not to increase their misery by denying them a Christian marriage again. For example, the Anglican tradition permits the re-marriage of divorcees at the discretion of the minister, who must gain approval from his or her bishop. In cases where this approval is not forthcoming, a blessing can be given after a civil ceremony. The Orthodox traditions have a unique, arguably ingenious, way of dealing with marital breakdown. The apostle Paul made it clear that the death of a spouse released the survivor to marry again (*Romans* 7:1–4). The Orthodox tradition has taken this release seriously and extended it to include not only physical but also 'moral death'. Thus if a couple can prove to the church's satisfaction that a marriage has irretrievably broken down, has died the 'moral death', then they are free to divorce and remarry without any disciplinary action invoked against them.

Historically Christians have tended to marry within denominational groups. The Roman tradition practices this endogamy (that is, marrying within a defined social group) and there are Protestant groups, for example, in Northern Ireland, which are firm in their closure of the group against outsiders. Groups such as the Amish who have settled in the USA also practise such endogamy. In the Roman tradition this approach is tied up with the idea that marriage is a sacrament and although it is acknowledged that the ministers of the sacrament are the couple themselves, and therefore an ordained priest is not strictly necessary for a marriage to be valid, the Roman Church has ruled that without the blessing of the church, in the person of a priest, such a marriage will not be considered regular. However, the Catholic Church will marry a Catholic to a non-Catholic Christian, as long as the non-Catholic partner agrees that any children will be raised as Catholics.

9.4.3 Contraception

Although in the 'catholic' traditions a contemporary awareness of the role of sexual relations has modified the language surrounding marriage, the Anglican and the Roman traditions differ radically as to the implications of such a reappraisal. Artificial means of contraception have been acceptable in the churches of the Anglican tradition since the 1930s. In the Roman Catholic tradition papal opposition to contraception is as solid as ever, and was reaffirmed by the publication of the papal encyclical *Humanae Vitae* in 1968 in spite of more liberal advice from a Vatican Commission. This strongly conversative position was also subsequently upheld by Pope John-Paul II during the 1980s and 1990s. In the contrast between the reactions of the two traditions it is interesting that they both turn to 'natural law' as the basis for their decisions. In the Anglican tradition the fact that the sexual act does not inevitably lead to conception and procreation, that it is pleasurable and can be enjoyed for most of the time without an end result being possible let alone denied, is an argument for facilitating its happening with the certainty, or at least the near certainty, that conception will not follow by employing artificial contraception. Allied to this is the view that it is responsible parenthood not to allow the conception of unwanted offspring.

In the Roman tradition the same natural law is used to emphasize the procreative view of sexual relations and to hold that nothing should be done to impede such procreation else it becomes an occasion of thwarting the will of God. The Roman tradition does allow the adoption of the 'rhythm method' whereby sexual relations are confined to the so-called 'safe period' during the menstrual cycle. It thus acknowledges that procreation is not the only legitimate reason for marital partners to have sexual relations. Catholic teaching will not allow the loop (Intra-Uterine Device) method of contraception. This does not inhibit the transmission of seminal fluid, but it will abort a fertilized egg. A casual glance at population statistics will reveal, however, that very many Catholics in Europe and North America cannot possibly be conforming to their church's teaching. Indeed, it is a grave matter of conscience to many such Catholics, and to the priests who hear their confessions (if they do confess their revolt), that they should continue to defy the church and that the priests should continue to give them absolution. Most Protestant traditions, in contrast, have not taken such a strong line on contraception. The tendency is to leave it to the individual conscience but generally to approve of responsible parenthood. There is more agreement between all the traditions, however, in the matter of our next topic, medical termination of pregnancy, otherwise referred to as abortion.

9.4.4 Medical termination of pregnancy

Christian moral opinion has always been against abortion, a practice that was especially prevalent during the first two centuries of the Christian era. Nevertheless it was not until fairly recently that the Roman tradition took the decision to condemn all forms of abortion. St Augustine made a distinction between an animate and an inanimate foetus, allowing abortion of the latter. Animation, literally the presence of an *anima* (soul), was taken to occur sixty to eighty days after conception. According to English law at one time there was a distinction to be made concerning the foetus before and after 'quickening', that is, the moment when the foetus is felt to move by the mother. Towards the end of the nineteenth century, however, the Pope ruled against abortion for any reason.

By contrast, while most Christian traditions maintain that artificial abortion is immoral and campaign for legislation against unlimited termination, some Christian traditions do allow it under certain conditions. One of the key areas of dispute between the Roman tradition and others is that Rome will not allow abortion even to save the mother's life. Only if a foetus is aborted indirectly through surgery or treatment for some other objective is it not a culpable act. (See, for example, *Reader* 2.18.) Other traditions will come down in favour of the mother's life where there is a clash between the interests of the foetus and of the mother. The area of debate from here on surrounds the definition of good cause for abortion. The threat to the physical life of the mother may be fairly easy to define, but what about the threat to the mother's mental and social well-being? Beyond this there continues the question as to the status of the foetus and the question of its viability outside the womb. In addition, as medical science advances and more is known about the condition of the foetus *in utero*, the question of the abortion of a malformed foetus becomes more and more problematic. In addition there is the question of what should be done in the case of the pregnancy of a rape victim and of girls who conceive under the age of consent. The debate ranges from those who maintain that after conception the foetus is an 'unborn child' and has the right to life however malformed it may be, to those who would distinguish a viable individual from a being who is not viable, and who may be faced with a future which will be less than dignified, and for those with responsibility to care for him or her.

Some Christians argue that the control science gives human beings over nature fulfils the *Genesis* command to 'subdue the earth', placing the responsibility on humanity to take decisions that balance the well-being of the mother, the foetus and society. There is no simple answer, however, and in an area of moral decision making in which emotions are easily aroused it is as well to realize that there are no simple answers.

9.4.5 Homosexuality

Homosexuality refers to a predominant and persistent psychosexual attraction felt by an individual towards members of the same sex. More recently the terms 'gay men' and 'lesbians' have come to be widely preferred by same-sex oriented individuals because of the negative and narrow associations of the term 'homosexuality' with genital activity. In fact, it is important to distinguish between same-gender attraction and same-gender sexual acts: the latter may be indulged in by heterosexuals on occasions and may be abstained from by celibate gay men and lesbians.

Traditionally what has been considered from the Christian moral point of view under the heading of homosexuality has been same-sex *acts*. The question of homosexuality as a personal orientation has only recently been a matter of debate, in response to general medical and psychological views. Thus there are those who consider homosexuality to be primarily a condition induced by social and environmental factors and take a strong stance against it, while on the other hand there are those who consider it to be a genetic or hormonal condition, and thus part of 'nature', and tend to take a more sympathetic attitude towards homosexual relationships.

It is the view of the majority of scholars that throughout history Christian authorities, initially under the influence of Roman law, have condemned homosexuality, but with varying severity. (For a contrary interpretation see Boswell, 1980.) Penalties proposed for infringement of the moral law have not been universally harsh. Graduations of gravity have sometimes been recognized with related graded penances. The whole subject has been influenced by Thomas Aquinas who held that the sexual organs should only be used in the interest of the generative process. As we have seen, that view is now challenged over a wide area of Christian ethics, and attitudes towards same-sex relations have changed in line with these new attitudes towards sexual relations generally. One Christian writer, accepting that homosexuality is part of nature, has suggested that:

> We now know new things and different things. We understand much better the process of reproduction; and we understand with far greater wisdom the sexual foundation of all human bonding and friendship. Moral judgement and advice cannot responsibly be formed as though such understanding had not been discovered ... Our ancestors got most of what matters right: fidelity and commitment, control and order are not being called into question. But our evaluation of sexual behaviour is profoundly affected by the changes in our understanding of what that behaviour is naturally, in nature.
>
> (Bowker, 1987)

The contrary argument drew attention to two different uses of the term nature. There was the scientific sense used in the above quotation, but there was a second sense:

> ... which is more valuable to the moralist. In this other sense we try to discern the character of a thing, and recognize its virtue in fulfilling that nature ... To see whether homosexuality is natural in this useful sense we should seek the aid of the more humane sciences: psychology, biography, art – for the question is not 'How does this occur?' but – 'Is this part of the good life for man?' Answering such questions is very much more difficult than reading off the putative conclusions of natural science, partly because it is in man's nature to be artificial and to learn a second nature of language, sensibility and custom; and partly because

> that second nature, including sexuality, is exceedingly flexible ... We may commend tolerance and sympathy, but shall not want homosexuality praised as part of a normal and natural way of life.
>
> (Target, 1987)

In the 1990s, the debate over homosexuality – and in particular the question of whether practising homosexuals may be ordained – has caused great controversy in the Church of England especially. A service held in Southwark Cathedral (Anglican) in November 1996, to celebrate twenty years of the Gay and Lesbian Christian Movement, once again stirred up controversy over the issue of gay and lesbian Christians. This subject is explored further in audio cassette 3.

10 Conclusion

Exercise

In the Course Guide you have been given three key questions around which it was suggested you should organize your study of all the religions in this course. Now answer these questions as they relate to the Christian religion, remembering the complexity and plurality of the different forms of the religion.

The three key questions are:

(a) What is the starting point of Christianity?

(b) What are the immediate and ultimate goals of Christianity?

(c) How does Christianity enable its followers to achieve their goals?

Discussion

(a) This question can have many answers. For example, a theological answer is in God's creativity in making the universe or in God's self sacrificial love shown in the incarnation, itself the means to effect a reconciliation between God and sinful humanity. An historical answer is in first century Palestinian Judaism, a corner of the Roman Empire.

(b) The immediate goal of life for the Christian is to do God's will, in the power of the grace of God, exercising love in all things. The correct action at any time has to be worked out on the basis of an awareness of the love of God and the influence of God on the individual conscience.

The ultimate goal or destiny is the establishing of the kingdom of God or the kingdom of heaven. This will come about according to God's will and the vocation of the Christian is to await the coming of the kingdom. In the kingdom the community will dwell in bliss with God: the eschatological vision in *Revelation* culminates in the heavenly city (*Revelation* 21:2).

(c) Christianity proclaims that salvation from sin and alienation from God has been made available to human beings through the life, death and resurrection of Jesus Christ, the Son of God and second person of the Holy Trinity. The church, referred to as the Body of Christ, has taken the major responsibility for spreading the Christian gospel. Divided throughout much of its history, the church in its denominational forms has various explanations of the saving work of Jesus Christ, and has understood its own role in significantly different ways. In responding through faith to the sacrifice of Jesus, Christians consequently rely on a range of means to realize their ultimate goal. For some the ritual of the sacraments provide a channel of grace; for others the study of scripture provides the basis for daily observance. While Christians may agree on the importance of following broad ethical teachings such as those contained within the Sermon on the Mount, there is considerable diversity in the working out of these broad principles in different contexts.

Summing up

In these two units we have looked at the Christian religion as it has developed in history and as it appears in the world today. For most of its history the Christian religion has enjoyed a superior, even imperial, position among the world religions in certain areas of the world. It is still the dominant influence in many societies, but it faces many challenges which occur in two major ways. There is the challenge of secularization, for example. Forecasts over the past century of the decline of religion in the face of secularization have been premature to say the least, and if closely scrutinized, grossly exaggerated. However, there is a sense in which secularization is influential if only in its alliance with democratization and the privatization of the individual's religious or philosophical tendencies. The picture of organized religion is patchy while personal religiosity may be more constant. Officially the Christian religion has still to face up to this particular challenge. In popular form, especially in such areas as the charismatic movement, and in such phenomena as television evangelists, the people are taking matters into their own hands. Another challenge to Christianity is from the newly emerging and increasingly proselytizing eastern and New Age religions. There are signs that the Christian religion is taking this challenge seriously at an official level, though quite how it meets the challenge is unclear. The Christian religion, which for centuries has been tolerant of the study of other religions, now has to face the hard fact that it could lose ground in its medieval heartland of Europe to religions that sometimes seem to offer better answers to the problems which beset our world and its future existence, while it continues to expand in other areas of the world.

11 Key issues

1 The person of Jesus: human or divine?
2 The gospels: biographies or theologies?
3 The different major traditions of Christianity: Catholic, Orthodox, Protestant – and also the variations and diversity within each of these traditions.
4 Key doctrines: creation, fall and redemption; the Christian hope of salvation; the atonement; the trinity.
5 Worship: its nature, its significance, its relationship to belief and practice, its variety; how it relates to and reflects the ethos of different branches of the Christian tradition.
6 Tensions: between doctrine and practice, between individual and community, between official and popular, between continuity and change.
7 Institutions, rituals and leadership.
8 The sources of ethical judgements.
9 Christianity in the modern world.

References

ASTON, M. (1981) 'Popular religious movements in the Middle Ages' in Geoffrey Barraclough (ed.) *The Christian World: a social and cultural history of Christianity*, London, Thames and Hudson.

BARTSCH, H.W. (ed.) (1972) *Kerygma and Myth: a theological debate*, second edition, London, SPCK.

BOSWELL, J. (1980) *Christianity, Tolerance and Homosexuality*, Chicago, Chicago University Press.

BOWKER, J. (1987) 'We must study creation to understand providence', *The Independent*, September.

BROWN, P. (1988) *The Body and Society: men, women and sexual renunciation in early Christianity*, London, Faber and Faber.

CONGAR, Y.M.J. (1939) *Divided Christendom: a Catholic study of the problem of reunion*, Geoffrey Bles.

DRURY, J. (1990) 'Parable' in R.J. Coggins and J.L. Houlden (eds) *A Dictionary of Biblical Interpretation*, London, SCM.

DUNN, J.D.G. (1980) *Christology in the Making*, London, SCM.

FIORENZA, E.S. (1983) *In Memory of Her: a feminist theological reconstruction of Christian origins*, London, SCM.

GUSTAFSON, J.M. (1978) *Protestant and Roman Catholic Ethics: prospects for rapprochement*, Chicago, University of Chicago Press.

MACINTYRE, A. (1981) *After Virtue*, London, Duckworth.

RICHARDSON, A. and BOWDEN J.(eds) (1983) *A New Dictionary of Christian Theology*, London, SCM.

STROUP, G.W. (1981) *The Promise of Narrative Theology*, London, SCM.

TARGET, L. (1987) 'Homosexuality is not part of the natural way of life', *The Independent*, 3 October.

WILES, M. (1976) *Working Papers in Doctrine*, London, SCM.

A213 World Religions

Units 1–2 Judaism

Units 3–4 Christianity

Units 5–6 Islam

Units 7–10 Hinduism

Units 11–13 Buddhism

Units 14–15 Sikhism

Unit 16 Religion at the end of the twentieth century

Study Guide 1 Sacred place

Study Guide 2 Women in religion

Study Guide 3 Making moral decisions